A Treasury of Magical Knitting

by Cat Bordhi

ALSO BY CAT BORDHI:

Socks Soar on Two Circular Needles: a Manual of Elegant Techniques and Patterns
Passing Paws Press, Inc, 2001

Treasure Forest, FIRST OF THE FOREST INSIDE TRILOGY
Namaste Publishing, 2003

A Second Treasury of Magical Knitting
Passing Paws Press, Inc., 2005

New Pathways for Sock Knitters, Book One
Passing Paws Press, Inc, 2007

ISBN 0-9708869-7-7

Book cover, design & layout: Bruce Conway, Lightwatcher (www.lightwatcher.com)

Photography:
Model, project, and technique photos by Michael Hopkins (mahphoto@comcast.net),
Nature shots and Shey the cat photo by Cat Bordhi,
Round hay bales photo on page 33 by Steve Brandt,
Topological offspring photo on page 101 by Bruce Conway.

Passing Paws Press, Inc
P. O. Box 2463
Friday Harbor, WA 98250

web site: www.catbordhi.com   email: cat@catbordhi.com

Printed in Manitoba, Canada by Friesens, Inc.

DEDICATION:

To the knitter who got lost and arrived late at a Magical Knitting Workshop, missing my introduction. Ten minutes later, as the room became enveloped in silence, each person lost in the

enchantment of effortless knitting, the lost knitter raised her head, her face now child-like. "Has anyone read *The Power of Now* by Eckhart Tolle?" she asked, "because that's what we're doing."

I gulped, because, yes, it is, although we need not say a word.

Welcome home.

ACKNOWLEDGEMENTS

I have many people to thank for helping with this book, but my biggest helper is not a person. During these months of swimming down the Moebius stream with wool and needles in hand, I have not really invented anything, or even been creative. Instead, one after another, knitted Moebius forms have risen to meet me as if they were already here, just waiting for someone to come and play with them. The forms have an elemental, primordial beauty which I could not have invented.

There are so many radiant people who have helped me bring these lovely knitted bits of grace to you. My workshop students always push windows open, inspiring me with fresh air and insights, and help me immeasurably as test knitters. Julie Taylor, owner of Island Wools in Friday Harbor, Washington, seems to always have the yarn I need, right here on our little island, and encourages me with a twinkle in her eye. My dear friend Sivia Harding understands and nourishes the very essence of creativity and knitting, and has been a wonderful parallel friend in the Moebius universe. My playful and talented book designer, Bruce Conway, danced like a Tai Chi master with the text and graphics and allowed me to be his apprentice; it has been so much fun we suspect it may be illegal. Jen Conway, Bruce's artist wife, keeps his feet in hand-knit socks, fills their home with her masterful knitting designs, and is an inspiration. The Skacel Collection, Crystal Palace Yarns, Honey Lane Farms, Mountain Colors, and Wool in the Woods have all been most generous in sending me delicious yarns for the projects in this book. I was most fortunate that Orell Russi, of Russi Sales, Inc, responded to my question about how to go about photographing this book myself by replying, "Let me call Michael." Michael Hopkins appeared ten minutes later, and saved me from mediocrity, as you will see in his stunning photographs. And my dear friend Kim Norton sailed over from Lopez Island with her fresh eyes to help proof the final pages, giving me wonderful last-minute advice, and picking up her knitting needles to check things out one last time.

In the middle of writing this acknowledgement page, my model, Vanessa Rose Ament, stopped by Bruce's office to see the book design. Afterwards she gave us a gift: she sang an aria from La Bohème. If I could include her voice in this book, it would outshine everything in its pages. Her voice is pure and powerful, rising out of her depths as if she were a flower who can sing. Vanessa had never modeled before, but I knew, from watching her on stage and having known her since she was a child, that she would embody the magical essence of this book. I cannot find words to express how grateful I am to her for being a part of this book's expression of the divine.

And now I hand everything to you, knitter-reader whose eyes are moving along this page. Everything divine in this book is yours, ready to rise through your heart and needles and gently startle you with its simple beauty. Through you, the beauty herein expands.

Table of Contents

*In magical knitting, thinking relaxes into "seeing". You allow yourself
to be carried forward, one stitch at a time, with no effort or worry.*

Magical Knitting Workshop student, Seattle, WA

INTRODUCTION

*W*elcome to the world of magical knitting, where graceful shapes flow from your needles – even if you're not quite sure how you got here from there.

I first encountered the form that inspired magical knitting while teaching elementary school, searching for ways to engage my youngsters with the beauty of mathematical shapes.

Once I brought this mysterious form into the classroom, it enchanted us all, and we spent hours exploring its nature. But we could only go so far, because we were making models with paper, pencils, scissors, and tape. It was not until years later, when I experimented with knitting this form, that it stretched and swayed and truly came to life, inviting me to enter its delightful dimensions with all my senses alert. After several years of playing with it, I can tell you it is mysterious and above all else, simple.

I'm going to introduce you step by step to this magical form as if you were one of my students. Later I'll tell you a story about the German man who discovered it over a century ago, and then you'll be ready to start knitting your first one.

Please find a pencil or pen, scissors, tape, and a sheet of blank paper.

Cut a long, narrow rectangle of paper.

Write "I love to knit because . . ." starting at the bottom left corner of the strip, along the bottom edge.

Hold the ends of the strip together so they resemble a ring.

Carefully turn one end over so that the "wrong side" meets the "right side." Tape the ends together.

Now finish writing your sentence about why you love to knit, staying right along the bottom edge. Keep adding reasons you love to knit until something stops you.

Can you figure out what happened?

How many *sides* are there on what only moments ago was an ordinary, two-sided strip of paper?

Now examine the *edge* of the twisted ring. What does your long "I love to knit because . . ." sentence reveal? How many edges are there?

The strip's two original sides have merged to become one side (one surface) and the two long edges are now one twice-as-long edge. Like magic!

Just for fun, try this: Can you color the paper blue on the outside and red on the inside? If you succeed, let me know, and I'll send you a prize.

Just wait until we apply these mysterious qualities to knitting. In the first *Treasury of Magical Knitting,* we'll knit scarves from the center out in one fell swoop, capes with transforming collars, hats with endless beginnings, and felted boots with no inside or outside, although your feet won't know it.

The Second Treasury of Magical Knitting expands on what you learn in this book, and is filled with felted and unfelted bags, baskets, bowls, and cat beds, which I'm sorry to say, also have no inside or outside, but your cat will not fall out of them.

Please join me now for a journey back in time to 1858, so you can meet the German mathematician who stumbled upon the wonders of this simple half twist and even had it named after him.

As far as I know, August Ferdinand Moebius did not know how to knit. Since the details have been lost in history, I would like to offer you a fictional recreation of the events which led to the book you hold in your hands. Please come with me to a candle-lit house on a cobblestone street in Leipzig, Germany, in the middle of the nine-teenth century, where we hear the whirring sound of a spinning wheel and the pacing of leather-clad feet.

August is anxiously watching his wife as she spins. "Can you finish in time? We have only four days left!"

"Mein Liebling," Helga replies. "Stop fretting. I'll be done spinning by the time we sit down to our Gulaschsuppe, and after supper I can finish knitting your scarf." She gazes at the long, thin piano wire knitting needles sticking out of her yarn basket. "If I ever have a moment's rest I'm going to carve a pair of shorter needles and glue a string between them. I saw it in a dream I had last night!"

"Forget your dream! What about my formula?" August asks, wringing his hands.

"The scarf shall be embroidered with your formula soon enough," Helga promises him, but she seems to be thinking of something else. "Maybe the violin maker down the alley can give me an old violin string and some good glue . . ."

Three days pass, and Helga is just about to sew the

equal sign near the end of the long formula which her brilliant husband is to present at the Leipzig Topologist's Symposium.

Suddenly August bursts out of his study, his hair wild and his eyes bulging. "Halt!" he cries, snatching the needle from his wife's hand.

"Is something amiss?" Helga asks him, retriev-ing her needle and calmly rethreading it.

August Ferdinand Moebius

"My formula is wrong!" August hands her a scrap of paper. "Add this before the equal sign!"

"Mein Liebling," Helga sighs, "I am so close to the end. There is no room to embroider these additional numbers. Luckily, I've been careful to keep my embroidery from showing through on the back. Shall I just continue the equation on the other side?"

August's sad eyes slowly grow bright. "Perhaps so! Perhaps so!" he cries, and lifts the beginning of the scarf, turning it over to the blank side, and holding it next to the other end. "Can you stitch the ends together?"

"My maiden name isn't Kitchener for nothing," Helga replies. A few minutes later she hands her husband a perfectly grafted scarf.

"It's like magic!" he cries. "Now you have twice the length to write out my formula!"

At the Leipzig Topologist's Symposium, August Moebius stands proudly on the stage, reading from the endless scarf around his neck. His colleagues are impressed by his mathematics, and enchanted by the single, continuous edge and surface of the mysterious scarf, which they agree to call a Moebius band.

Meanwhile, Helga decides to knit a second Moebius scarf using the circular needle she has fashioned from carved wood and an old cello string (for a violin string was too short to travel around the single edge of the shape). You see, she'd had a second dream in which the mysteries of what we call magical knitting were revealed, and she discovered how to do a Moebius Cast-on.

Helga knit by candle-light until her death in 1901. She never quite caught up with all the orders for Moebius scarves which she received from topologists from all over Europe.

The violin maker, who believed that one of the magical scarves would bring him good fortune, carved her a special set of circular needles out of a broken Stradivarius violin and connected them with the finest bass cello string he could obtain. And August never grew tired of watching his wife create her own versions of the form which bears their last name to this day.

Alas, none of the Moebius children, a daughter and two sons, wished to carry on the Moebius knitting tradition, so the needles and Moebius techniques died with Helga. Later generations of topologists and school children all over the world have used paper, scissors, and paste instead of needles and wool to make and investigate Moebius bands. And there is only so much you can do with paper, because it doesn't stretch.

Now, so many years later, the knitting that might have flowered on this branch of mathematics is ready to burst into full bloom as you, dear knitter, play with the patterns and ideas in this book.

Supposing my tale were true (and I must confess that to my impressionable mind it feels true), I find myself wondering if Helga Moebius might have set down the daily sock-knitting many women did at that time, and begun knitting Moebius scarves? After all, in addition to magic and mystery, they also promise down-to-earth practicality (they never fall off and hang gracefully no matter what). I think she would have.

Following in the imaginary footsteps of our Helga, that is just what I have done. I set aside my sock-knitting (I wrote *Socks Soar on Two Circular Needles,* published in 2001) and fell in love with magical Moebius knitting. This book contains the best of my discoveries.

In the next chapter you will learn the Moebius Cast-on, as it came to Helga in her dream. It opens the door to everything in both *Treasuries.* Once you learn to do it, the wonders of Moebius-land await you.

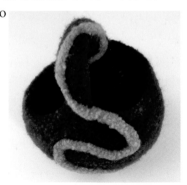

Swirl Moebius Basket,
Second Treasury of
Magical Knitting

This is what I've been waiting for! A way to knit a real Moebius that works!
Magical Knitting Workshop student, Gig Harbor, WA

What's the big deal about Moebius knitting? You just knit a long rectangle, twist one end, and graft them together. Or is there something I don't know?
an uninitiated knitter

CHAPTER ONE — TECHNIQUES, AND ONE TOOL

In 1858, when Helga knit her Moebius scarves, she had to not only invent circular needles, but invent one with a long enough string, or cable, to make it possible to knit a Moebius in the magical way. She only grafted one Moebius scarf in her life – the one with August's formula on it. After that, she used her cello-string device to knit Moebius scarves in one fell swoop, just as we are going to. Something as flowing and graceful as a Moebius ought not to be interrupted by a seam.

I'd like to dispel a myth believed by many knitters somewhat familiar with Moebius scarves, who think they have knitted them on needles as short as sixteen inches.

Circular knitting instructions usually warn against twisting the stitches when joining. But if this dreaded twisting occurs, the curled piece of knitting you end up with is *not* a Moebius. If you've done the paper and tape exercises in the introduction, you may understand why this cannot be true.

A twisted line of stitches, joined and knit upward, has two separate edges – one cast-on (the bottom) and one bound-off (the top). It cannot be a Moebius, which has only one edge. In addition, this sorry

Moguls Moebius Scarf, page 35

piece of knitting will be found to have two sides, twice as many as the mysterious Moebius. It also has a 360° (full) twist instead of a 180° (half) twist. And it will not fall very gracefully, with such a lot of twist.

Elizabeth Zimmermann was the first person to introduce the charm and wonders of the Moebius to knitters, in her book, *Knitting Around*, in 1989. If you read her narrative, you'll feel her excitement, and see that she, too, quickly determined that this form could not be knit by simply twisting a join. Instead, she grafted a rectangular strip with a half-twist, thereby eliminating one surface and one edge. Her beautiful scarf has inspired thousands of knitters, and her graft is no doubt impossible to find. However, this practical method does not lead to the delightful knitter's playground of our magical one-fell-swoop Moebius.

When you knit a Moebius in one continuous flow of stitches, you find beautiful patterns emerging naturally and symmetrically from the center out, with very little effort or attention on your part. Since you have only one edge to finish, you'll never have a bound-off side tighter than the cast-on. And you'll never find your cast-on at all, because it's swallowed up in the center of the scarf. Beginning and end are swallowed up as well.

But most of all, and this is hard to explain, there is simply a joy and peacefulness in allowing the true Moebius to do all the work for you. You'll have to find this out for yourself, by knitting one.

ONE EDGE, ONE SURFACE, & ONE TOOL

A long circular needle between 47" and 60" long is probably the only tool you need to buy for knitting the designs in this book. Addi Turbo needles, both metal and bamboo, are available in these lengths, Crystal Palace bamboo needles come in a 55" length, and you can purchase a Denise Needle Kit with additional longer cables which will give you all the sizes you need to knit everything in both *Treasuries*. Your knitting will be a little slower with the Denise needles because the cable is thicker, and you will have to frequently push your stitches around the long path they follow.

Why do you need such a long needle? Because it will work in a coiled position, like so:

The needle tips must to be able to work together, and shorter needles simply do not offer enough cable length

There's enough cable on this 47" needle to allow the tips to interact easily.

to permit them to work together. It is *possible* to use a 36" or 40" length to knit a Moebius, although they will push back against you, and if you have joint problems or arthritis, you should definitely not attempt a Moebius with this shorter length. I recommend them only for the hats, which are best done on a 40" needle. If you already have a 60" needle, you'll find it will work fine for everything in this book except for the hats and the felted boots.

THE MOEBIUS CAST-ON (MCO)

THE FASTEST IN THE WORLD

The Moebius Cast-On (the MCO) you are about to learn may be the fastest cast-on in the world, once your hands learn the simple moves. In my workshops I like to demonstrate it behind my back just to let people know that it is pretty easy.

TWO SIMPLE MOVEMENTS TO REPEAT:
One: scoop a loop from under the cable.
Two: scoop a loop from over the cable

The photos show the step by step process.

STEP ONE

Make a slip knot and place it near one end of the cable, as shown. The needle closest to the slip knot hangs down and is ignored until you have finished casting on. The other needle does the casting-on. Note that the needles are pointing in opposite directions.

STEP TWO

This is "home" position, and shows how you hold the yarn, cable, and needle. Your right thumb and middle finger pinch the slip knot and cable. Your right hand also holds the working needle. The yarn runs behind the cable and is tensioned in your left hand. Your left thumb and middle finger pinch the cable as shown.

STEP THREE

Here we go. The needle dips down in front of the cable.

STEP FOUR

The needle goes under the cable and comes up in the triangle between the cable and the yarn.

STEP FIVE

The needle rises up from the triangle.

STEP SIX

The needle swoops *over* the top of the yarn and down behind it, ready to scoop a loop and bring it "home".

STEP SEVEN

The needle has scooped a loop and is bringing it back under the cable, retracing its earlier path, "home" to the space between you and the cable (as shown in step 2).

Step Eight

The needle reaches up *over* the top of the yarn, ready to scoop a loop.

Step Nine

The needle is scooping a loop. Notice it has reached up, *over*, and behind the yarn to scoop the loop.

Step Ten

The needle has re-traced its path and is bringing the scooped loop "home."

I suggest you practice the MCO for several minutes until it is second nature, like knitting or purling or riding a bike.

Counting MCO stitches

Now that you've practiced the MCO, I'll teach you how to count your stitches correctly, and have you practice the MCO once more while you count out loud.

Count each scoop as one stitch. Notice that for every two stitches you scoop, two matching stitches appear on the cable beneath the needle. You will be knitting these lower stitches, but *do not count them when you cast on* or you will end up with half as many stitches as you need! Only count the scooped stitches, which are on top.

See the four stitches on the needle? These are the stitches you count – they are the loops you scooped.

Check for one crossing
of needle and cable

If you have more than one crossing of cable and needle, your Moebius will be a tangle instead of a graceful flow. Spread the stitches so they reach from one needle to the other as shown below. You will have to pull or push the cables and needles to get them into position.

Think of the cable and needle as a train track. If a train is to travel these tracks, they must be parallel, like the l's in the middle of the word, parallel. Press the cables flat and parallel starting from the left needle all the way around to the

cable and needle cross here

right needle. Along the right needle your train will derail – for the tracks should cross once here. If they cross more than once, rotate the right needle around the cable until there is just one cross. It is rare to have more than one cross, but you must always check to be sure you don't. I learned the hard way! Note: Your crossing may be either cable over needle, or needle over cable.

KNIT YOUR FIRST STITCH

Now place a marker on your right needle (mine is beaded). Insert your needle through the loop of the slip knot and knit your first stitch.

JUST SAY NO TO THOSE LEAPING FROGS

On the first round, when you try to push the stitches up the left needle so they can be knit, the stitches tend to leapfrog over one another and make it hard to slide them along. Spread them apart one by one, and push them up the needle one at a time.

The first half round is awkward, because the needle and cable are wrapped so close together. Soon they will begin to spread apart as your rounds of knitting grow between the needles and cables.

FIRST HALF ROUND

On the first half round, the stitches are mounted alternately, so that you must knit one through the back loop, the next through the front loop, and so on.

Knitting into the back loop of a stitch.

Knitting into the front loop of a stitch

SECOND HALF OF ROUND

Continue knitting alternately through back and front legs until you find your marker dangling on the cable *beneath* your needles, *where it cannot be removed*. You are halfway around the single continuous edge. From this point on the stitches will all be mounted normally. You may notice purl bumps along the entire needle and be quite sure you have knit one full round – but actually you are only halfway around. Take a look and you'll see there are no purl bumps on the other side of the needle yet.

KNIT THE NEXT STITCH

Knit into the stitch formed by the side of the slipknot. The slip knot itself is below, on the cable beside the marker.

Continue knitting until the marker finally appears in between your needles, where it could fall off if you aren't careful. Notice that now there are purl bumps on both sides of the needle all the way around.

CONGRATULATIONS!

You have completed your first round.

You may see a bit of a gap where your yarn tail is. Once you've completed the scarf you can use the tail to weave the gap together. As for the slip knot, in all the scarves I've knit, I have never once noticed the knot in a finished scarf, and you probably won't either.

STITCHES ARE GROWING
BETWEEN YOUR CABLES

Believe it or not, you are knitting your Moebius band from the "spine," or center line, out. Each time you complete one round, two rounds of stitches show up between the parallel cables. If you were to suddenly change colors, you would have a stripe on both sides of the spine after completing one round! I told you this was magic!

YOU'RE READY TO BEGIN

At this point you have the skills to begin your first project. For a while, you will probably wonder what you are doing and how it will turn out. Don't worry. To succeed, you only need to knit each stitch as it rotates into place between your needles. And every stitch will arrive, endlessly and in perfect sequence, until it is time to bind off. There are no forks in the simple road of magical knitting, so you cannot take a wrong turn. You're home safe.

It's a miracle that simply knitting along, la-dee-dah, turns into this beautiful Moebius.
Magical Workshop student, Menlo Park, CA

CHAPTER TWO — SIMPLEST-OF-ALL MOEBIUS SCARF

It wasn't until this book was almost finished that I decided I'd better check that something I'd been telling my Magical Knitting Workshop students was actually true. You see, if you just knit every stitch of a Moebius as it rotates into place between your needles, which every stitch will do without any effort on your part, it ends up as something that one of my students, Morgan Hicks of Seattle, cheerfully labeled "Bipolar Stockinette": all stitches to the right of the Moebius spine will look knit (right side stockinette) and those to the left will look purled (reverse stockinette).

I didn't think that sounded very appealing, so I'd always steered students to the Purl Ridge Scarf which you'll find in Chapter Two.

But when I actually tried knitting a "Bipolar Moebius," to my surprise I discovered it was blessed with a special grace. And to think I had rejected it sight unseen! It makes me wonder what else I've missed out on.

And so I encourage you to try the newly christened "Simplest-of-All Moebius Scarves." I show it in three very different yarns to give you some sense of its range.

CHOOSING YARNS FOR MOEBIUS SCARVES

If you'd like a lively scarf that sways as you move, look for yarns that have some weight to them, like alpaca, rayon, silk, linen, lustrous wools, and some synthetics. You can also use two strands of yarn, one of them with good drape, the other one less so. When you knit your swatch, keep going up needle sizes until your fabric is as drapey as you wish. If you'd like your scarf to nestle against you, and stay put, try yarns that are bulkier, fluffier, or a little firmer. When in doubt, go up a needle size, since in general a scarf ought to be loose enough to have some movement.

In the yarn information for each pattern, I include the "wraps per inch" (wpi) of the yarn so you can compare the diameter with other yarns. To measure the wpi of any yarn, simply wrap it around a ruler and gently push the strands together until they cover one inch. The number of wraps in one inch is your wpi. Wrapping a thick rubber band around the ruler at each side of one inch will help make your count more accurate, so that you are sure you are covering exactly one inch.

I recommend you make a gauge swatch approximately 6" wide and 4" inches high. Your swatch will tell you if your fabric feels right, and also give you the number of stitches-per-inch of knitting so you can determine how many to cast on.

HOW MANY STITCHES SHOULD YOU CAST ON?

I've provided a table on page 20 so you needn't calculate the number of stitches to cast on for knitting a Simplest-of-All Scarf, but it's very simple to do yourself. Just hang a tape measure

How many stitches to cast on for a Moebius Scarf

Circumference	32"	40"	48"	56"	80"	
1.5	48 sts	60 sts	72 sts	84 sts	120 sts	
2	64 sts	80 sts	96 sts	112 sts	160 sts	
2.5	80 sts	100 sts	120 sts	140 sts	200 sts	
3	96 sts	120 sts	144 sts	168 sts	240 sts	
3.5	112 sts	140 sts	168 sts	196 sts	280 sts	
4	128 sts	160 sts	192 sts	224 sts		Believe me, you don't want to knit such a lot of stitches at this fine gauge.
5	160 sts	200 sts	240 sts	280 sts		
6	192 sts	240 sts	288 sts	336 sts		
7	224 sts	280 sts	336 sts	392 sts		

Gauge: (stitches per inch in 1 row)

around your neck to decide how many inches around you'd like your scarf to be, then multiply that number by your stitches-per-inch gauge. This is the number of stitches to cast on using the Moebius Cast-On which you learned in chapter one.

How many stitches you cast on determines the *length* of your scarf, while the number of rounds you knit gives you the *width*. You simply knit until your scarf is wide enough, then bind off. It's that easy.

HOW MUCH YARN WILL YOU NEED?

This will vary depending on your gauge and the weight of the yarn. The easiest way to estimate

yardage is to simply check the yarns used in the pattern as given. If your own yarn can be knit at about the gauge of the pattern yarn, you can buy approximately the same yardage.

A handy way to determine the yardage needed of any yarn is to decide how wide and long you want your scarf to be, and to figure the square inches (width of scarf multiplied by length of scarf = square inches of knitted fabric necessary). Then unravel your 6" x 4" gauge swatch and measure the yarn used for its area, which is 24 square inches. If the gauge swatch is not 6" x 4", measure it carefully before unraveling, and multiply its length and width together to determine its square inches. Divide the number of square inches in your gauge swatch into the square inches of your desired scarf, and multiply the answer by the length of yarn you used to knit the gauge swatch. Add another 10-20 yards tothe answer just to be safe.

Now here's the first pattern in the book, in generic form, so you can use it for any yarn. Refer back to the techniques taught in the previous chapter as needed. At the end of the generic pattern you'll find specific directions for each of the scarves pictured.

Simplest-of-all moebius scarf
Basic Version

Here is the simplest of all possible Moebius knitting:
Cast on, knit, knit, knit, and bind off.

Yarn: Choose any yarn you like.
Needles: 47" - 60" circular in the size that gives you a desirable fabric with your chosen yarn.
Notions: tapestry needle, stitch marker

Gauge: Determine your gauge in stockinette stitch by measuring how many stitches are in a row 4" (10 cm) wide. Divide by 4 for sts per inch.
Stitch guide: See page 111 for abbreviations.

How many stitches should you cast on?

Just drape a tape measure around your neck and hold the ends together at the circumferences in the chart on page 20. A 48" scarf is ideal: long enough to coil twice around your neck, or to wrap your neck once and also go over your head like a hood. Choose the circumference you like and find the number of stitches to cast on for your stitch gauge. If your gauge is in between those given, choose a cast-on number in between the two gauges. For this scarf, an exact number is not important at all.

Review techniques in previous chapter as needed.

Beginning
MCO the desired number of stitches.
Place marker on right needle tip.
Continue
Knit until the scarf is as wide as you want it to be, plus one to two inches, because the edge will roll in.
Bind off
Bind off loosely. To insure you are binding off loosely enough to match the drape of your fabric, bind off 4" - 6" and let it hang to see if it is loose enough. If not, bind off with a larger needle, or use this elastic method of binding off: Knit 2, * replace 2 sts on left needle and knit them together from right to left through the back loops, k1, repeat from *. Weave in all ends.

THE SNUGGLER

*If this is your first Moebius scarf, the bulky
yarn will make it go quickly. This was the first
"Bipolar Stockinette" scarf I tried, and its
beauty showed me right away that I had
indeed missed the boat by steering everyone
away from such a simple, graceful design.*

Yarn: Lana Grossa Caldo Print
(98% wool, 2% nylon binder cord,
100g/ 65 yds, 3.5 wpi),
#12 moody blues, 3 balls
Needles: (you may require a different
size to get correct gauge) size 13 (9 mm)
circular, 55" - 60" length
Notions: tapestry needle, stitch marker
Gauge: 8 sts = 4" (10 cm)
Finished size: circumference 45",
width 8"
Stitch guide: See page 111 for
abbreviations.

Beginning
MCO 90. Place marker.
Middle
Knit 14 rounds.
End
Bind off loosely.
Finishing
Weave in ends and block if desired.

FRINGED CEDAR BARK SCARF

The native people who lived for thousands of years in the Pacific Northwest used cedar bark to weave clothing, and this scarf seems to glow with the same sun-kissed texture. In my workshops people take turns wearing it because they all fall in love with it.

Yarn: Colinette Giotto (50% cotton, 40% rayon, 10% nylon, 100g/ 144m, 5-6 wpi), #76 lichen, 1 skein

Needles: (you may require a different size to get correct gauge) size 11 (8mm) circular, 47 - 60" length, medium crochet hook

Notions: tapestry needle, stitch marker

Gauge: 10 sts = 4" (10 cm)

Finished size: circumference 40", width 8"

Stitch guide: See page 111 for abbreviations.

Beginning
MCO 100. Place marker.

Middle
Knit 16 rounds.

End
Bind off loosely. Weave in ends.

Finishing
Cut about 100 eight inch pieces of yarn for fringe. Attach the fringe every other bound-off stitch: fold a piece of yarn in half, insert crochet hook through a bound-off st, and pull loop end of yarn halfway through. Pull cut ends of yarn through loop and pull tight. Repeat all the way around, every other stitch.

Swinging Mikado

This feather boa of a Moebius will nestle around your neck and you won't be able to keep your hands off it. Take it dancing! I've added an additional step to this scarf - you will purl the final three rounds. Don't care for purling? Switch direction and knit the final three rounds, and you'll get the same effect.

Yarn: Crystal Palace Fizz (100% polyester, 50g/ 120yds, 15 wpi) #9154 Sage Mix, 1 ball; Crystal Palace Mikado Ribbon (50% cotton, 50% rayon, 50g/ 112 yds, 8 wpi) #2679 green, 2 skeins
Needles: (you may require a different size to get correct gauge) size 13 (9 mm) circular, 47" - 60" length
Notions: tapestry needle, stitch marker
Gauge: 6 sts = 4" (10 cm)
Finished size: 6" wide, 86" circumference
Stitch guide: See page 111 for abbreviations.

Beginning
MCO 130. Place marker.
Middle:
Knit 8 rounds. Purl 3 rounds.
Finishing: Elastic bind-off: Knit 2, * replace 2 sts on left needle and knit them together from right to left through the back loops, k1, repeat from * to end, and weave in yarn ends.

Yarn and design suggestions: Try these scarves in any yarn you like, and find out what happens. You can always unravel. At a workshop in Vancouver, British Columbia, one knitter tried knitting a very wide ribbing – perhaps k8, p8, along the edge, and it gave a ruffled effect. Soon other knitters were copying her! Or try attaching fringe down the bipolar spine instead of at the edges – play!

How do you block a Moebius?

You cannot lay a Moebius flat on any surface in your house. However, a pile of towels over the end of the ironing board will suspend your Moebius, so the twist can hang below. You can redampen and pin out the surfaces as they take turns rotating every few hours to the top, until everything is lovely. Or, you can use my favorite system for nearly everything in this book: don't bother blocking it! A nice shot of steam iron is usually enough.

CHAPTER THREE – PURL RIDGE MOEBIUS SCARF

A Moebius scarf will stay put in a windstorm, and always drape beautifully, flowing around your neck with the sort of graceful curves we normally associate with a stream of water or honey. So here's another basic design for you to try. The Purl Ridge Scarf is nearly as mindless as the Simplest-of-All Scarf, and so beautiful that I happily knit a dozen in a variety of sensual yarns before it occurred to me to explore other designs. One day I was wearing my own favorite, done in Mountain Colors Moguls, when a businessman passed me in a bakery doorway, then wheeled around. "That's a fantastic scarf!" he shouted, and set out into the rainstorm.

HERE ARE THE BASIC DIRECTIONS:

Step 1: Do a Moebius Cast-on.

Step 2: Knit for 1, 2, or 3 rounds.

Step 3: Purl the same number of rounds as above.

Step 4: Repeat steps 2 and 3 until your scarf is wide enough.

Step 5: Bind off.

Moebius Purl Ridge Scarf
Basic Version

I suggest you read through this pattern before moving on to the featured designs, because it is full of instruction.

Yarn: enough for length and width you wish (see page 20)
Needles: 47" - 60" length circular in size to give good drape with your yarn
Notions: tapestry needle, stitch markers
Gauge: Determine this by knitting a swatch in stockinette stitch. If you plan to knit 1 round, purl 1 round for steps 2 and 3, then work your gauge swatch in garter stitch (knit all rows).
Finished size: see chart on page 20 for circumference choices; width is determined by how many rounds you knit.
Stitch guide: See page 111 for abbreviations. See "How many stitches should you cast on?" on page 20 or the chart on page 20 to determine how many stitches you will need.

Step 1:
Work Moebius Cast-On (MCO) for desired number of stitches. Place stitch marker on right needle tip. Knit until marker reappears *between* the needles (*not* on the cable below - this position indicates you are just halfway around the single edge). Now it's time to make a decision. Do you want the purl ridges on your scarf to be one, two, or three rounds wide? I almost always work three-round ridges, except when I use a highly textured yarn, and then I work one-round ridges.

Step 2:
You've decided how many rounds you want your ridges to be, so knit one, two, or three rounds. Don't forget you have already completed your first round.

Step 3: Purl rounds: purl until your marker reappears on the needle, signaling you have purled one full round. Purl the same number of rounds as you knit in step two.

Step 4: Continue knitting, then purling your chosen number of rounds until the scarf is as wide as you'd like.

Step 5: There are two very satisfactory ways to bind off. The simplest is to bind off loosely, which will give you a narrow rolled edging with a reverse stockinette surface. Make certain to bind off loosely using a larger needle if needed, or use the elastic cast-off: Knit 2, * replace 2 sts on left needle and knit them together from right to left through the back loops, k1, repeat from *.

My own favorite edge finish is applied I-cord. We will use this technique in many designs in both *Treasuries*, and I will teach it to you next.

HOW TO WORK APPLIED I-CORD

FIRST ADD 2 STITCHES USING THE KNITTED CAST-ON

Step 1: Knit 1 stitch but do not move the completed stitch to the right needle as you normally would.

Step 2: Slip the new stitch onto the left needle. Twist the stitch before slipping it over the left needle tip.

Step 3: Knit 1 stitch in the twisted stitch on your left needle tip, but do not move the completed stitch to the right needle.

Step 4: Instead, slip it onto the left needle tip, twisting it as in step 2. You now have 2 new stitches on your left needle, both twisted. You have done the Knitted Cast-On, and set yourself up to start the Applied I-Cord.

START APPLIED I-CORD

Step 5: Knit 3 stitches.

Step 6: Replace the 3 sts you just knit back onto the left needle. Your working yarn is coming from the back of the 3rd stitch.

Step 7: Knit 2 stitches, pulling the yarn up from the bottom of the 3rd stitch.

Step 8: Knit the next 2 sts together from right to left, through the back loops.

Repeat steps 6-8 until all stitches are bound off.

Ideally you would graft the ends of the I-cord together, and I will show you how. But if this seems like more than you want to do, simply sew the ends together, mimicking knit stitches as best as you can.

Grafting I-cord ends

Step 1: Insert a knitting needle at I-cord beginning, through a row of 3 knit stitches. Cut a tail of working yarn and thread it through a tapestry needle.

Step 2: Insert tapestry needle through first loop on lower needle as if to purl. Pull yarn through.

Step 3: Insert tapestry needle through first loop on upper needle as if to knit. Pull yarn through.

Step 4: Insert tapestry needle behind next 2 loops on lower needle. Pull yarn through.

Step 5: Insert tapestry needle through first loop on upper needle as if to purl, and take loop off needle. Pull yarn through.

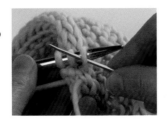

Step 6: Insert tapestry needle through first loop on upper needle as if to knit. Pull yarn through.

Repeat steps 4 - 6

Step 7: Remove upper needle, and insert tapestry needle through last stitch on lower needle from left to right. Pull yarn through. Remove lower needle.

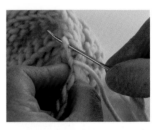

Step 8: Insert tapestry needle through final edge stitch that was on upper needle, as if to purl. Pull yarn through.

Step 9: Insert tapestry needle through final edge stitch that was on lower needle. Pull yarn through. Give the join a tug to pull the stitches neatly into alignment. Now weave the tail in and cut the end.

TO GRAFT I-CORD WITH MORE THAN 3 STITCHES, SIMPLY REPEAT STEPS 4-6 FOR THE EXTRA STITCHES.

MERGING STRIPES

Yarn: Heirloom 8-ply (100% wool, 50g/ 98m, 13 wpi) #791 green, 2 skeins; and 1 skein each of #789 brown, #725 beige, #785 blue

Needles: (you may require a different size to get correct gauge) size 15 (10 mm) circular 47" – 60" length

Notions: tapestry needle, stitch marker

Gauge: 11 sts = 4" (10 cm)

Finished size: 48" circumference, width 4.5" unstretched, 8" stretched

Stitch guide: See page 111 for abbreviations. Work with 2 strands of yarn throughout. The green yarn is joined in turn by beige, blue, and brown.

Beginning

MCO 130 with beige and green held together. Place marker. Knit 3 rounds. Purl 3 rounds.

Middle

Cut tail of beige, add blue to green. Knit 3 rounds. Purl 3 rounds. Cut tail of blue, add brown to green. Knit 3 rounds. Purl 3 rounds.

End

With green and brown held together, work applied I-cord to finish edge (see page 28-29).

Very bouncy and springy, this Moebius even looks great wrapped twice around your head like a hat! It also demonstrates how one yarn color can blend with others when worked as two strands held together. The base color of green underlies the transition between beige, sky blue, and brown so that they seem to change slowly. Notice the mirror reflection of color changes – if you hold a mirror along the spine of the scarf you can view an image of both sides!

SHIFTING COLORS MOEBIUS

This scarf, like Merging Stripes, also has merging stripes! In this case, however, the yarn does the colorwork for you. Noro Kureyon has very long color repeats, which show up in the scarf in a less precise mirror reflection than the Merging Stripes Scarf, because the Noro changes are not as regular. The color you cast on with will appear in the center of the scarf, as the brown does in this one.

Yarn: Noro Kureyon (100% wool, 50g/ 100m, 8 wpi), #115 red/brown/green, 2 skeins.
Needles: (you may require a different size to get correct gauge) size 13 (9 mm) circular 47" – 60" length
Notions: tapestry needle, stitch marker
Gauge: 10.5 sts = 4" (10 cm)
Finished size: 50" circumference, width 5" un-stretched, 8" stretched
Stitch guide: See page 111 for abbreviations.

Beginning
MCO 130. Place marker.
Middle
*Knit 3 rounds, purl 3 rounds.
Repeat from * 3 times.
End
Work applied I-cord (see pages 28-29) or simply bind off loosely (or use the elastic cast-off: Knit 2, * replace 2 sts on left needle and knit them together from right to left through the back loops, k1, repeat from *).

HONEY LANE ALPACA

This lovely hand-painted alpaca comes from Honey Lane Farms on the island where I live. The yarn is luxuriously soft and warm, and has marvelous drape. To make this longer than average scarf shorter, just cast on fewer stitches.

Yarn: Honey Lane Farms Alpaca Hand-Paint (100% Alpaca, 100 g/ 220 yds, 13 wpi), watery blue colorway, 3 skeins

Needles: (you may require a different size to get correct gauge) size 8 (5 mm) circular 47" length

Notions: tapestry needle, stitch marker

Gauge: 16 sts = 4" (10 cm) after blocking

Finished size: 55" circumference; width unstretched 5.5", stretched 10"

Stitch guide: See page 111 for abbreviations.

Beginning
MCO 220 sts. Place marker.

Middle
*Knit 3 rounds. Purl next 3 rounds. Repeat from * until desired width is reached.

Finishing
Work applied I-cord (see pages 28-29) to finish edge and weave ends together. Weave in all yarn ends.

HAY BALE MOEBIUS

On the San Juan Islands the hay is put up in enormous round bales that dot the pastures every summer. The flat ends of the bales spiral like whirlpools of yellow and remind me of the buttery stripes that curve around this Moebius scarf.

Yarn: Crystal Palace Cotton Chenille (100% cotton, 50g/ 98 yds, 7.5 wpi), #9113 gold, 1 skein; Crystal Palace Merino Frappe (80% Merino wool, 20% polyamide, 50g/140 yds, 8 wpi), #061 yellow, 1 ball
Needles: (you may require a different size to get correct gauge) size 13 (9 mm) circular 47" – 60" length
Notions: tapestry needle, stitch marker
Gauge: 9.25 sts = 4" (10 cm)
Finished Size: 56" circumference, width 6" unstretched, 9" stretched
Stitch guide: See page 111 for abbreviations.

Beginning
MCO 130 with Merino. Place marker.
Middle
Knit 3 rounds. Cut tail of Merino. With Chenille, p 3 rounds. Cut tail of Chenille. With Merino, k 3 rounds, then p 3 rounds. Cut tail of Merino. With Chenille, k 3 rounds, then p 3 rounds. Cut tail of Chenille.
Finishing
With Merino, work applied I-cord (see pages 28-29) and weave ends together. Weave in all yarn ends.

MOGULS MOEBIUS SCARF

In the winter this is the Moebius scarf I reach for nearly every time I go out the door, and the wider version is my ice skating scarf, because it really keeps me warm. I start out with it wrapped around my neck and pulled over the top of my head, and as I warm up I release it to fly behind me. I show this scarf in three colorways and two widths.

Yarn: Mountain Colors Moguls (98% wool, 2% nylon binder cord, 100g/ 65 yds, 4.25 wpi), 1 (2) skeins; Mountain Colors 4/8's Wool (100% wool, 100g/ 245 yds, 11 wpi), 1 skein

Needles: (you may require a different size to get correct gauge) size 11 (8 mm) circular 47"– 60" length

Notions: tapestry needle, 2 stitch markers

Gauge: 8.5 sts = 4" (10 cm) in Moguls

Size: 48" circumference; width is either 6" (1 skein Moguls) or 10.5" (2 skeins Moguls), not counting fingers, which add another 2" to each scarf.

Stitch guide: See page 111 for abbreviations.

Beginning

MCO 100 sts. Place marker.

Middle

Knit 1 round, p 1 round. Repeat these 2 rounds until you run out of Moguls.

Border

With double strand of 4/8's Wool, place new marker (remove original one when you come to it) and work an increase round: *k1f&b, k1, repeat from * all the way around. You now have 300 sts total. *Purl 1 round, k 1 round, repeat from * once.

Fingers

Remove marker. *Add 5 sts using a knitted cast-on (see page 28). Bind off those 5. Bind off the next 5 edge stitches. Replace final bound-off st on left needle. Repeat from * until all sts are bound off. Weave in ends.

Ladyslipper - Two Skeins Moguls

Northern Lights - Two Skeins Moguls

Golden Willow - One Skein Moguls

Cloud Stream Edged in Blue Sky

This gentle scarf has slowly increasing bands of puffy purl ridges growing from its center – three rounds wide, then four, then five. The subtle change gives a sense of shifting presence, like clouds in the sky. If you'd like to make the scarf wider, purchase additional cream yarn and keep adding wider bands of knit and purl rounds.

Yarn: Honey Lane Farms Alpaca (100% alpaca, 50g/ 110yds, 13 wpi), cream, 2 skeins, clearwater, 1 skein

Needles: (you may require a different size to get correct gauge) size 11 (8 mm) circular 47" – 60" length

Notions: tapestry needle, stitch marker

Gauge: 14 sts = 4" (10 cm)

Size: 48" circumference; width is 3.5" unstretched, or 7" stretched

Stitch guide: See page 111 for abbreviations.

Beginning

With cream, MCO 165. Place marker.

Middle

Knit 3 rounds. Purl 3 rounds.

Knit 4 rounds. Purl 4 rounds.

Knit 5 rounds. Purl 5 rounds. Cut tail of cream.

Finishing

With blue, work applied I-cord edge (see pages 28-29) and weave ends together. Weave in any loose yarn ends.

Sandstone and Sky Felted Stripes

Introducing the glories of felting!

Here is a scarf that has been lightly felted in the washing machine. Even if you've never felted before, this is a great first project. In fact, the resulting fabric is so captivating that I often pick this scarf up and begin dreaming of an entire

jacket or vest made of it. It is soft and pliant, like a baby's blanket.

How do you felt? Just knit the scarf, and then put it inside a pillowcase and secure the top shut with one of those big rubber bands that come on broccoli. You want to protect your washing machine from swallowing too much fiber fluff. In Vancouver, British Columbia, long ago, a company that did commercial carding of fleeces actually stopped up the Vancouver sewer system after many months of sending fluff down the drain. Your washing machine feels the same way. So keep that fluff in the pillow case.

Just fill your washing machine with hot water to the low water setting. Add a little bit of laundry soap – about a quarter of what you'd normally use. Add a few other things to bat the pillowcase around (jeans, tennis shoes, or what I use, a half dozen big rubber bouncy balls) and set the dial to agitate. Because the scarf only needs to shrink a little, check it every two minutes. Take it out as soon as the colors merge enough to blur the purl bumps that show on one side of a color change.

Gently rinse the scarf in warm water (not cold, or it will shrink more), and either put it through the spin cycle or just go outside and spin it wildly around your arm, sprinkling the lawn and your dog and making it necessary to wash your windows again. It's more fun to do this but easier to put it through the spin cycle. Then push, pull, and pat the scarf flat and beautiful and lay it somewhere to finish drying, perhaps over the end of the ironing board so the Moebius twist can hang free.

Take a look at the scarf. The raised ridges have flattened and the lines of purl color change have merged so that they scarcely show. You have created a whole new fabric. If this is your first felting experience, welcome to what may become your new addiction.

The Second Treasury of Magical Knitting will be full of bags, bowls, baskets, and beds for you to felt, and of course, they are all Moebii.

Here's the pattern for your first felted Moebius:

Yarn: Lana Grossa Royal Tweed (100% Merino Fine, 50 g/ 100m, 9 wpi) #13 sandstone, #18 sky, 2 balls each
Needles: (you may require a different size to get correct gauge) size 10.5 (7 mm) circular, 47"– 60" length
Notions: tapestry needle, 2 stitch markers
Gauge: 14 sts = 4" (10 cm) before felting
Finished size: 12" wide and 58" circumference before felting; 7" and 48" after felting.
Stitch guide: See page 111 for abbreviations.

Beginning
With Sandstone, MCO 170. Place marker.
Middle
Knit 510 (1 full round of 170 + 170, plus a half-round of 170). Place new marker here, and remove the first one when you come to it again. *You have established a new beginning point with the new marker.* *Cut tail of Sandstone. With Sky, p 4 rounds. Cut tail of Sky. With Sandstone, k 4 rounds. Repeat from * once. Cut tail of Sandstone. With Sky, p 4 rounds. Cut tail of Sky. With Sandstone, k 3 rounds, then *purl 1 round, k 1 round, repeat from * once.

Finishing
Bind off loosely. Weave in ends. Felt according to directions above. Do not over felt!

Yarn and design suggestions
Different yarns felt at different rates. This could be desirable or not – if you want a flat scarf, use two colors of the same yarn (and be sure any yarn you use is close to 100% wool, mohair, llama, or alpaca, and not super-wash, or it won't felt). But if you'd like a seersucker effect, use two yarns which felt at very different rates. There is no end to new things to try in knitting, no matter how long you live.

I don't know what it is about the knitted Moebius, but it keeps recreating itself — there's definitely on-going energy — in perpetual motion.
artist viewing the Magical Knitting collection, Vancouver, British Columbia

CHAPTER FOUR – MERCURIAL SHAPES

*A*mong the greatest joys of designing are those sudden Eureka! moments when a window swings open to reveal a whole new realm of possibility. One day a window blew open to show me that the Moebius scarves wanted to leap out of the straight sides I'd kept them in so far, and swell and curve and swim. It's just a matter of sequencing increases on one side of the spine and decreases on the other.

The first "Shaped Moebius" I made was so mesmerizing that I vowed I'd never make a straight one again. Well, I was wrong – but as you will see, these shaped Moebii are absolutely enchanting and they fall in the most unpredictable ways.

I actually came up with the name of the second wrap in this chapter – the Mercurial Moebius – very late one night in December while staying in West Seattle with Virginia Bowen, owner of the Seattle Yarn Gallery, where I was teaching workshops. My students had been urging me to write a book about the magical knitting they were learning, and that night I decided that indeed I would write this book.

I actually had an Ott light beside my bed (such luxury!) and until the wee hours I kept having to hop up and turn it on and write down or draw the designs that were flooding through my head. It was like one of those newsreels of the

Mississippi River flooding, with cows and houses and bicycles charging downstream, only in this case it was one Moebius after another rushing through my consciousness.

The only problem was that I had no paper in my possession other than a few receipts I dug out of my purse. My notebook was out in my car, which was covered in a light dusting of snow when I peeked out the window in the moonlight, and I didn't dare get up and creep around the house and wake people up. So I was recording my ideas in tiny writing with tiny drawings and soon my receipts were filled, but my Mississippi mind continued to flood with one Moebius after another! So I peeked into the closet and found an old school binder with some paper inside and gingerly removed a few pages.

By morning I had over one hundred potential Moebius designs and was weary but blissful. I'd gotten quite a bit of exercise in the dead of the night, with all that hopping up and down.

Towards the end of the Moebius flood, I'd begun to play with the sound of the words themselves. The "Mercurial Moebius" was a lullaby to my tired ears – and you'll find it in this chapter. Think of mercury and how spontaneously and freely it moves – so does this wrap.

There is another Moebius from that late night flood that I still want to make, but I'm not sure if you'd like it. It's the "Moth-Eaten Moebius" and I'll give you the directions right here just in case. It is best to embrace your fears, you know, or in this case, let them embrace you.

Moth-Eaten Moebius

Knit an extra big and very loose Moebius scarf on large needles, with wool that will felt. If you make mistakes, all the better. Holes in your knitting or dropped stitches? You're on the right track. In case you don't have any dropped stitches, snip the yarn here and there before dropping it into a washing machine full of nice hot soapy water, or throw it in the tub with your three rambunctious toddlers and let them have at it. When it is suitably felted, take it out and examine it. The holes ought to have opened up just enough while felting to resemble moth holes! If you like, felt some moth-colored wool, cut out moth shapes, and sew them near the holes. Wear with pride, and please send me a picture.

Mohair Moebius Scarf-Shawl

This beautiful shawl was conceived weeks later, after I had caught up with my sleep. It has no moth holes, but is airy and full of light and warmth. Anita and Missy are the two wildly creative and gloriously funny women who create hand-dyed yarns at Wool in the Woods in Pennsylvania. They sometimes teach color workshops which are not to be missed. I look forward to seeing them every year at a trade show. This inviting wrap is a favorite among my workshop students — one pattern everyone requests. Make sure you have the loose gauge the pattern calls for.

Yarn: Wool in the Woods Miss Mohair (78% mohair, 13% wool, 9% nylon, 200 yd skeins, 8 wpi), High Sierra colorway, 1 skein; Wool in the Woods Cherub (100% wool, 200 yd skeins, 12 wpi), Poppy Patch colorway, 1 skein. *Note: yardage is very close; you may want additional yarn. If you buy two skeins of Miss Mohair, the applied I-cord edging can be done with two strands of this yarn. This would assure you of having enough yarn.*

Needles: (you may require a different size to get correct gauge) size 15 (10 mm) circular 47" - 60" length

Notions: tapestry needle, 10 stitch markers, one white, the rest colored

Gauge: 7.5 sts = 4" (10 cm)

Finished Size: approximately 48" circumference (measured around spine), and 11" wide

Stitch guide: See page 111 for abbreviations. You must have exact stitch count in order to place the knit and purl sections correctly. If you are off by just 1 to 3 sts, increase or decrease as needed on the first round, placing the increases or decreases at the edge of a knit-purl change. If you are off by more, why not start fresh?

Beginning

MCO 90. Place white marker.

Middle

Round 1: *Knit 18 sts and place a colored marker. Purl 18 sts and place a colored marker, repeat from * 4 times. On the last repeat you will come to the white marker so do not need to place another marker. *Note: Your 5th colored marker is placed directly above the white marker, signaling that you are now halfway around the first round. After this, each new marker is placed directly above a previous marker. As you continue to knit and the cables spread apart, so will the markers.*

Round 2: *Knit to next marker, p to next marker, repeat from * 4 times.

Round 3 - 4: Repeat rounds 1 and 2.

Round 5: K2tog, k16, *p2tog, p16, k2tog, k16, repeat from * once; m1p, p18, *M1R, k18, m1p, p18, repeat from * once.

Round 6: K17, *p17, k17, repeat from * once; p19, *k19, p19, repeat from * once.

Round 7: K2tog, k15, *p2tog, p15, k2tog, k15, repeat from * once; m1p, p19, *M1R, k19, m1p, p19, repeat from * once.

Round 8: K16, *p16, k16, repeat from * once; p20, *k20, p20, repeat from * once.

Round 9: K2tog, k14, *p2tog, p14, k2tog, k14, repeat from * once; m1p, p20, *M1R, k20, m1p, p20, repeat from * once.

Round 10: K15, *p15, k15, repeat from * once; p21, *k21, p21, repeat from * once.

Round 11: K2tog, k13, *p2tog, p13, k2tog, k13, repeat from * once; m1p, p21, *M1R, k21, m1p, p21, repeat from * once.

Round 12: K14, *p14, k14, repeat from * once; p22, *k22, p22, repeat from * once.

Round 13: K2tog, k12, *p2tog, p12, k2tog, k12, repeat from * once; p22, *k22, p22, repeat from * once. *(Second half of this round is not increased.)*

Round 14: K13, *p13, k13, repeat from * once; p22, *k22, p22, repeat from * once.

Round 15: K2tog, k11, *p2tog, p11, k2tog, k11, repeat from * once; m1p, p22, *M1R, k22, m1p, p22, repeat from * once.

Round 16: K12, *p12, k12, repeat from * once; p23, *k23, p23 repeat from * once.

Round 17: K2tog, k10, *p2tog, p10, k2tog, k10, repeat from * once; p23, *k23, p23, repeat from * once. *(Second half of this round is not increased.)*

Round 18: K11, *p11, k11, repeat from * once; p23, *k23, p23, repeat from * once.

Round 19: K2tog, k9, *p2tog, p9, k2tog, k9, repeat from * once; m1p, p23, *M1R, k23, m1p, p23, repeat from * once.

Edging

You will work a 4-stitch applied I-cord edging. Using knitted cast-on (see page 28), cast on 4 sts. *Knit 3, k next 2 sts together from right to left tbl. Slide the first 4 sts on the right needle back to the left needle. Pulling yarn snugly behind, repeat from * to end until all sts have been worked. Graft or carefully sew I-cord ends together (see page 29) and weave in yarn ends.

Yarn and design suggestions

You may use any yarn, provided you can get the same gauge in a fabric you like. I knit mine with two strands, mohair and a soft, lightweight yarn, but it could certainly be knit in a single heavier strand. Or, use three beautiful yarns held together – anything that matches the large, loose gauge. You could also use multiple yarns from your stash, and vary their placement for a stunning effect. Intarsia doesn't suit a Moebius, because of the single side offering nowhere to hide the "wrong side," but you might play with duplicate stitch streaks or stitch motifs with special yarns, like eyelash, or bouclé, or other textured, showy yarns. You can also work multiple applied I-cord rounds, stacking them up for extra width. Simply pick up the stitches along the edge and keep knitting.

MERCURIAL MOEBIUS WRAPS

Here is the wrap that came to me towards the end of the midnight flood – actually just the name came, but swimming inside the tantalizing sound of the name was a Moebius just like this. You may knit either one or two. I had intended to use the two to create a Moebius vest, but it simply didn't work out as I'd hoped. Tantalized by much experience with mistakes-turned-fruitful, I began playing with the pair and discovered they were delicious heaped one on top of the other. Just throw one on, then the other, allowing them to fall into original grace without much manipulation. If you wear a pair, you'll begin to wonder why you always thought you needed a coat with sleeves. I have worn them instead of a coat even in the winter, here in the Pacific Northwest. If you want to knit just one, you will need only two skeins of Mountain Colors Moguls instead of four.

Yarn: Mountain Colors Moguls (98% wool, 2% nylon binder cord, 100g/ 65yds, 4.25 wpi), 4 skeins; Mountain Colors 4/8's Wool (100% wool, 100g/ 250yds, 11 wpi), 1 skein; Mountain Colors Mohair (78% mohair, 13% wool, 9% nylon, 100g/ 225yds, 8 wpi), 1 skein; all in Missouri River Blue colorway

Needles: (you may require a different size to get correct gauge) size 13 (9 mm) circular 47" - 60" length

Notions: tapestry needle, 2 stitch markers in contrasting colors

Gauge: 9 sts = 4" (10 cm) in Moguls

Finished size: circumference around spine 45", width 9.5"

Stitch guide: See page 111 for abbreviations.

If somewhere during the knitting of this wrap you find your stitch count is off by 1 or 2 sts, just correct it by either skipping an increase or decrease, or adding one. No one will ever know with this highly textured yarn.

Beginning
MCO 100 sts. Place first marker.
Round 1: Knit 100 sts, place second marker (a different color than the first), k 100 sts.
Middle
Round 2: Purl to first marker.
Round 3: Knit to first marker on this and all odd rounds.

Round 4: *Purl 18, p2tog, repeat from * 4 times, (second marker is here) *p 19, p1f&b, repeat from * 4 times, (first marker is here)

Round 6: *Purl 17, p2tog, repeat from * 4 times, (second marker is here), *p 20, p1f&b, repeat from * 4 times, (first marker is here).

Round 8: *Purl 16, p2tog, repeat from * 4 times, (second marker is here),*p 21, p1f&b, repeat from * 4 times, (first marker is here).

Round 10: *Purl 15, p2tog, repeat from * 4 times, (second marker is here), *p 22, p1f&b, repeat from * 4 times, times (first marker is here).

Round 12: *Purl 14, p2tog, repeat from * 4 times, (second marker is here), *p 23, p1f&b, repeat from * 4 times, (first marker is here).

Round 14: Purl to first marker.

Round 15: Knit until you run out of your second skein of Moguls. If you still have more, you may begin purling the next round. It doesn't matter where you run out.

Border

Use 2 strands of 4/8's held together with 1 strand of Mohair to p 1 round, k 1 round, and p 1 round. Next round: *Knit 3, yo, repeat from * to end, finishing with k2, k2tog, yo. You have 266 sts.

Finishing

Cut mohair and continue with 2 strands of 4/8's. *Bind off 3, k and bind off 4 more in the yo, (leave the yo on left needle until you have k and bound off all 4 sts that you work in it), repeat from * to 1 st before end, bind off final st. Weave in ends.

Note: I had designed this border with a row of yo holes so that sections of the two wraps could be woven together with knitted I-cord, or attached with

buttons. Who knows, you might want to play with the two and see what you can come up with. The holes are there waiting to be used, or to simply act as a decorative border.

Make a second Mercurial Moebius

Make another just like the first. If you are very particular and would like the two Mercurial Moebii to mirror each other in direction of twist, here is how: When you finish the MCO and check for twist, have the cable cross over the needle for one Mercurial Moebius, and under for the second Mercurial Moebius. (If you plan to try to use the two together as a vest of some sort, you'll want them to mirror.)

Yarn and design suggestions

Mountain Colors Moguls is a sensual, lumpy-bumpy yarn that comes in gorgeous, nature-inspired colorways. Seek out bulky, textured yarns alive with color. Do make sure to match the gauge fairly closely. If you use a very drapey yarn, like a bulky rayon or silk (that sounds wonderful!), you may want to go down in gauge, as the weight of the yarn will stretch the piece. You could also add fringe, or fingers (see the finishing section for the Moguls Moebius Scarf in chapter three). By the way, I often wear two or three Moguls Moebii together, in different colors – they all seem to work together and piled high they look fabulous – and are indescribably cozy.

Scottish Wave Scarf

The inspiration for this scarf came from Lois Slotemaker at Ana-Cross Stitch in Anacortes, Washington. She'd knit a rectangular scarf of these colors, using a variation of the Feather and Fan stitch, as I have. The yarns, which have a surprising variety of colors plied into a red or charcoal base, were stunning together. I made the transformations necessary for the scallops to become a Moebius, which meant an odd number of repeats, and reversed the direction of knitting halfway through to balance the design. Your stitch count must be precise, but you have until the end of round 8 to adjust, since the actual patterning begins on round 9.

Yarn: Tahki Shannon (100% wool, 50 grams/ 92 yds, 10 wpi) #14 red blend, #11 charcoal blend, 2 balls each

Needles: size 9 (5.5 mm) circular needle 47" - 60" length

Notions: tapestry needle, stitch markers

Gauge: 20 sts = 4" (10 cm) in stockinette

Stitch guide:

See page 111 for abbreviations. Remember that when you do the MCO, you only count the stitches that line up on the top needle, not those on the cable below (see page 15). This is why you can cast on 170, increase 1 st at the end of the round, and end up with 341 sts, which is 170 + 170 + 1.

Finished size: circumference 40", width 11"

Beginning

With charcoal, MCO 170. Place marker.

Round 1: Knit.

Round 2: Purl until 1 st before marker. Purl in front and back of last st to increase 1 st. (341 sts)

Middle

Round 3: Knit.

Round 4: Purl. Cut tail of charcoal.

Round 5: With red, *k2tog, k2, k1f&b twice, k3, ssk, repeat from * 30 times.

Round 6: Knit.

Repeat rounds 5 and 6 five times. Cut tail of red.

Round 17: With charcoal, knit.

Round 18: Purl.

Repeat rounds 17 and 18 three times.

Round 25: Knit. Cut tail of charcoal.

Turn work, so that you are heading in the opposite direction.

With red, repeat rounds 5-16. Cut tail of red.

Edge

Rounds 38-40: With black, k 3 rounds. Bind off using the elastic bind-off: Knit 2, *replace 2 sts on left needle and knit them together from right to left through the back loops, k1, repeat from *. Weave in all ends.

Yarn and design suggestions

One feature that makes this scarf so appealing is the bits of color common to both the red and charcoal yarns. And of course, red and charcoal set each other off in a wonderfully Scottish way. You might look for two variegated yarns that complement each other, or perhaps work the garter stripes in mohair and the other stripes in a complementary lustrous yarn like rayon or silk for a completely different look. You might also like to work some increases in the last three rounds, at the top of each scallop, to open and heighten the curves of the hem.

There's linear logic in straight needles, and circular logic in circular needles, but this is something different. It's getting your mind to dance in space, and it feels fantastic.

Magical Knitting Workshop student, Anacortes, Washington

Chapter Five – Mirrored Diagonals

You're about to "double your money" as you knit the designs in this chapter. For the "price" of knitting a simple diagonal line of yarn-overs, you'll create a mirror reflection of that diagonal line – and it will become an arrow design, growing from the spine of your Moebius. Yet this intricate-looking scarf has only two pattern rounds to repeat!

It's essential to start with an exact stitch count for the designs in this chapter, so turn off the phone while you cast on and establish the first round. Many of my workshop students have found it helpful to place a marker between each pattern repeat until they become more obvious.

Before beginning this scarf, make a paper Moebius (see page 7) and draw a line around the spine (the midline lengthwise). Now draw diagonal lines from the spine out to the right edge and continue around until you meet your first line again. Examine the other side of the paper, where your diagonal reverses all by itself (if you hold the paper up to the light, you can see the arrow pattern better). This reveals how your arrow will magically appear. The Moebius form is very generous with its gifts, and this is one of them.

Arrow Lace Pathways Scarf
Basic Version

As every surface in my home became draped with Moebius scarves during the writing of this book, this design always ended up on top because I love to look at it. Once the pattern is established, you'll be amazed at how the stitch marker slowly floats to the right with your diagonal, allowing the intricate pattern to consist of just one fourteen-stitch repeat. If you don't care for the long fingers along the edge, you can shorten them into little decorative nubs instead.

Materials: Cascade Yarns Pima Tencel (50% Pima cotton, 50% Tencel, 50 g/ 109 yds, 13 wpi), #4084 leaf green, 2 skeins

Needles: (you may require a different size to get correct gauge) size 7 (4.5 mm) circular 47" – 60" length

Notions: tapestry needle, stitch marker(s)

Gauge: 14 sts = 4" (10 cm) in Arrow Lace pattern after blocking

Size: 49" circumference, 6" wide without edging; 8 1/2" wide with edging.

Stitch guide: See page 111 for abbreviations. To make gauge swatch, cast on 28 sts to a circular needle and work 2 repeats of rounds 1-2 below (it is a 14 st repeat, so 28 is 2 repeats) back and forth as *rows*, not rounds, as follows: Work round 1, slide work back to other end of circular needle and bring yarn loosely from far end of work into position to knit round 2. Keep lengths of yarn loose across back of work so they do not pull it in. Continue knitting repeats of these two "rounds" (which you are knitting as rows) until swatch is about 4" high. Block swatch, perhaps over tip of ironing board, so strands can hang below, and measure for gauge in the middle. Or - don't worry about being so precise - after all, this is a scarf and need not fit like a sweater.

Beginning

MCO 168 sts. Place marker, and begin Arrow Lace pattern:

> Round 1: *P1, k1, p1, k1, p1, k9, repeat from * to marker.
> Round 2: *Yo, p1, k1, p1, k1, p1, k2tog, yo, p5, k2tog, repeat from * to marker.

Middle

Repeat rounds 1 and 2, finishing with a round 1 when you reach 6" or desired width.

Edging

Pick up 1 st in 1 of the strands of the yo stretched between your needles. *Bind off picked up st and next 7 sts. Slip final bound-off st from right needle to left needle, and use knitted cast-on (see page 28) to make 9 cast on sts from this stitch (see note below). Bind off 9 sts you just made, knitting into back loop of each stitch as you prepare to bind it off. Pick up 1 st in one of the strands of the yo stretched between your needles, and bind off remaining st from working the finger. Repeat from * until you have worked all the way around the edge.

Note: If you'd like shorter "fingers", work fewer cast-on and bound-off sts – anything from 2 (which will give you a little nub) on up.

Finish

Weave in ends and block scarf (do not neglect the blocking as the lace requires it).

MULBERRY SILK PATHWAYS SCARF

This was my original Arrow Pathways Scarf, knit with a luscious yarn Cascade Yarns sent me several years ago. Its high silk content would have made a most interesting and durable sock yarn, but it blossomed into this exquisite scarf instead. And now the yarn is no longer being made, so you'll have to look on eBay. Although you may have to choose a different yarn, you can see what the scarf looks like at a finer gauge than the basic version on the previous page. Just match the wraps per inch of your yarn with the yarn in this pattern.

Yarn: Cascade Yarns Success (50% Alpaca, 50% Mulberry Silk, 50g/ 123yds, 14 wpi) #613 pink, 3 balls

Needles: (you may require a different size to get correct gauge) size 5 (3.75 mm) 47" – 60" length

Notions: tapestry needle, stitch marker(s)

Gauge: 15 sts = 4" (10 cm) in Arrow Lace pattern after blocking

Finished Size: 49" circumference, 6" wide without edging; 8.5" wide with edging.

Stitch guide: See page 111 for abbreviations. See basic version for gauge instructions.

Beginning
MCO 196 sts.

CONTINUE WITH ARROW LACE PATHWAYS MOEBIUS SCARF – BASIC VERSION (PAGE 49)

BEADED TRESSES ARROW SCARF

You'll find the pattern for the Beaded Tresses Hat (which is so striking, you may not have noticed the matching scarf yet . . . we are still in a scarf chapter) on page sixty-six in the hat chapter. Which came first, the chicken or the egg? In this case, the hat, which garnered such enthusiasm from knitters who saw it that I knew it deserved a matching scarf.

Yarn: Skacel Incanto (35% cotton, 30% acrylic, 23% linen, 12% rayon, 50 g/ 95 m, 11 wpi) #03 lapis, 2 balls; # 02 coral, 1 ball

Needles: (you may require a different size to get correct gauge) size 7 (4.5 mm) 47" – 60" length

Notions: tapestry needle, stitch marker(s)

Gauge: 14" = 4" (10 cm) in Arrow Lace pattern after blocking

Finished Size: 49" circumference, 6" wide without edging; 8 1/2" wide with edging

Stitch guide: See page 111 for abbreviations. See basic version for gauge instructions.

START WITH COLOR LAPIS AND FOLLOW ARROW LACE PATHWAYS SCARF –BASIC VERSION (PAGE 49), MAKING COLOR CHANGES AS INDICATED.

Middle
Change to coral for last 4 rounds before edging.

Edging

Continue working with coral.

Yarn and design suggestions

If you wish to make the scarf longer or shorter, add or subtract 28 stitches from the MCO at a time. This is because the Moebius nature of the scarf requires an even number of repeats for correct placement along the spine, and a single repeat is 14 stitches. If you were to add 14 sts, the even number I have established would then be odd, so you have to add 2 repeats at a time instead, which is 28 sts. You could make a lovely shorter Moebius – something that would lie around your neck like a loose, lacey collar – with an MCO of 84 or 112 stitches (6 or 8 repeats).

Choose yarns which allow you to show off the Arrow Lace pattern – in other words, fairly smooth and not wildly variegated yarns, which may obscure stitch patterns. I plan to try one in Euroflax linen, another in a cotton-rayon blend, and maybe someday, Qiviut!

You could also make the scarf wider so that it is more of a shawl-wrap, or add beads to the little fingertips. I've often thought of running several strands of complementary yarn through the yarn-over holes and knotting the ends into fringe instead of knitting the little fingers. This is a playful scarf – have fun being creative with the basic design.

If you want more mirroring diagonals, there's one appearing as the scarf-collar of the Rimrock Cape in Chapter Nine. Feel free to simply knit the scarf and complete the edging, ignoring the cape directions.

A note for the inquisitive knitter: It *is* possible to knit a diagonal line which remains diagonal *almost* all the way around the Moebius, not becoming an arrow – until it inevitably collides with itself to make a series of stacking arrowheads!

I love how the lace motifs arrange themselves perfectly around the Moebius. Somehow it reminds me of birds flying in formation.

Magical Knitting Workshop student, Friday Harbor, WA

CHAPTER SIX – LACE REFLECTIONS

A Moebius scarf lends itself naturally to lace, for even the simplest lace becomes elegant when it blossoms into a mirror reflection of itself. Here you will find two airy shoulder wraps knit in summery fibers. Should you wish a winter Moebius lace wrap, both patterns will do just as well in wool, alpaca, silk, or another warm fiber.

Like the rather lacy diagonal scarves in the previous chapter, you must begin with a precise stitch count for these patterns to come out right. So give yourself uninterrupted time to establish the pattern in the first few rounds. You may want to place a marker between each pattern repeat until they look familiar to you.

Both wraps are shown worn as shoulder wraps, but look beautiful worn as scarves as well.

White Lacy Shoulder Wrap

This lightweight Moebius wrap will keep your shoulders warm on a balmy night. The yarn has a pearly, luminous quality that makes it look like an heirloom even before it comes off the needles. I give the pattern in four sizes so it will fit many different shapes of women.

Yarn: Skacel Riviera (45% cotton, 30% linen, 25% rayon, 50 g/ 110 yds, 17 wpi) #03 pearl white, 3 (3, 4, 4) balls

Needles: (you may require a different size to get correct gauge) size 7 (4.5 mm) circular 47" – 60" length

Notions: tapestry needle, stitch markers

Gauge: 18 sts = 4" (10 cm)

Finished size: 38" (42", 46", 50") circumference and 12" wide after blocking

Stitch guide: See page 111 for abbreviations. When the scarf is about halfway done, you will turn your work around to head in the other direction, moving your starting place over by 5 sts. This places the lace motifs between the earlier ones, creating a staggered effect.

Beginning
MCO 170 (192, 214, 236). Place marker.

Middle
Round 1: Knit to marker.
Round 2: Purl until 1 st is left before marker, p1f&b to increase 1 st.
Round 3: Knit.
Round 4: Purl. *This completes 4 rounds of garter stripe. Round 5 begins 12 rounds of lacy stripe.*
Round 5: *Knit 2tog, k3, yo, k1, yo, k3, ssk; repeat from * to marker.

Round 6: Knit to marker.
Rounds 7-16: Repeat rounds 5 and 6 five times.
This completes the lacy stripe, and now come 8 rounds of garter stripe.
Rounds 17-24: Repeat round 4 once, then rounds 3 and 4 three times, then round 3 once.
This completes 8 rounds of garter stripe, and the inner half of the scarf.

Outer half of scarf

Rounds 25-36: Turn work, so that you are heading in the opposite direction. Remove marker, k 5, and replace marker on right needle. *You have shifted your starting point.* Repeat rounds 5 and 6 six times. *You have completed the second lacy stripe.*

Finishing the edge

Round 37: Purl 5, p1f&b, p4, p2tog, *p4, p1f&b, p4, p2tog, repeat from * to marker. To complete final p2tog, move marker so you can p tog st before and st after marker, then replace marker on right needle after p2tog has moved there.
Round 38: *Knit 4, yo, k1, yo, k4, ssk, repeat from * to marker.
Round 39: Purl to marker.

Round 40: Knit 5, *yo, k1, yo, k11, repeat from * to marker, end k7.
Bind off loosely (or use the elastic bind-off: Knit 2, * replace 2 sts on left needle and knit them together from right to left through the back loops, k1, repeat from *). Weave in ends, and block.

Yarn and design suggestions

This wrap would be lovely done in a luxury yarn like cashmere or fine handspun. The lace motifs are large enough to show up in a variegated yarn as well. Think about working the garter stripes in a contrast color yarn for a very different look, or adding fringe. To make the wrap narrower, work fewer lace pattern repeats for each lace stripe, and to make it wider, add more lace pattern repeats for each stripe.

SAGE RHYTHM WRAP

This may be worn as a scarf or a shoulder wrap, and comes in three sizes to fit a variety of people. If you've never worked needle-wrapping before, you'll find it peaceful and rhythmic, for it has a little musical beat of its own: 2-2, 3-3-3, 4-4-4-4, 3-3-3, 2-2. The resulting lacy design flows in waves that flow over waves, like a slow dance – hence the name of this wrap: Sage Rhythm Wrap. Vanessa Rose Ament, my model, who is a divine singer and dancer, particularly loved this piece and asked me to make her one to wear for performances.

Yarn: Skacel Evita (40% cotton, 40% acrylic, 20% rayon, 50 g/ 110 m, 12 wpi), #10 sage, 3 (4, 5) balls

Needles: (you may require a different size to get correct gauge) size 9 (5.5mm) circular 47"– 55" length, medium crochet hook

Notions: tapestry needle, marker

Gauge: 13 sts = 4" (10 cm) in garter stitch (knit every row of your swatch)

Finished sizes: circumference 36" (44", 52"), width without fringe 9.5"

Stitch guide: See page 111 for abbreviations. As you insert the tip of the right needle and wrap the tip with yarn twice, 3 times, or 4 times, then pull the wraps through, all those wraps line up and crowd right needle's cable, because you have more than doubled the number of strands ofs yarn it holds – but just for this pattern round. On the next round you'll find the wrapped stitches tumbling off the left needle and you will have to "catch" them on the right needle. Be sure to knit (or

purl) each wrapped group as a single stitch. Once you have a whole section of wrapped stitches knit (or purled), it's fun to give them a tug so they stretch into the wave shape. You'll be surprised at how rapidly this wrap grows in width.

Beginning

MCO 117 (143, 169) sts. Place marker.

Middle

Rounds 1-2: Knit odd rounds, purl even rounds.

Round 3: *Knit 6; k 2, wrapping yarn twice around needle each time, k3, wrapping yarn 3 times around needle each time, k4, wrapping yarn 4 times around needle each time, k3, wrapping yarn 3 times around needle each time, k2, wrapping yarn twice around needle each time, k6. Repeat from * to marker.

Rounds 4-7: Purl even rounds, knit odd rounds.

Round 8: *Purl 2, wrapping yarn 4 times around needle each time, p3, wrapping yarn 3 times around needle each time, p2, wrapping yarn twice around needle each time, p12. Purl 2, wrapping yarn twice around needle each time, p3, wrapping yarn 3 times around needle each time, p2, wrapping yarn 4 times around needle each time Repeat from * to marker.

Rounds 9-12: Knit odd rounds, purl even rounds.

Rounds 13-22: Repeat rounds 3-12.

Bind off

Use this elastic bind-off: Knit 2, * replace 2 sts on left needle and knit them together from right to left through the back loops, k1, repeat from *. Weave in all ends.

Fringe

Cut approximately (125, 150, 175) 9" lengths of yarn. Fold yarn in half, and pull loop end through bound-off stitch with crochet hook, then pull the ends snuggly through fringe loop. Attach fringe to every other stitch all the way around.

Yarn and design suggestions I keep imagining beads strung in the lace windows, or swinging from the ends of the fringe. The wrap would also be wonderful in a fine bouclé, a drapey rayon, a kid mohair, or a hand-painted yarn – the possibilities are endless, and with all that air the knitting goes so fast! If you want to make the wrap wider, repeat rounds 5-9 once for another 2", or rounds 5-14 for another 4".

I be styling while I'm flying with my Beaded Tresses Hat! a snowboarder

CHAPTER SEVEN – MOEBIUS-BANDED HATS

*I*magine a Moebius scarf sized to fit your head, its magical twist signaling that it's more than an ordinary ski headband. But instead of leaving the top of your head out in the cold, stitches rise from the upper "edge" of the Moebius to form the crown.

The headband, or hat-band, can be worked as any scarf in this book (except for the shaped ones), just in a smaller circumference.

And of course, if you'd like to make a Moebius ski headband, you don't have to knit the top; just finish the edges of the small scarf and you're done. If you'd like to be a designer, this is a great place to dive in!

The Jeweled Merino Cap begins as a Simplest-of-All Scarf. The Reversible Lotus Blossom was briefly incarnated as a Purl Ridge Scarf, and the Beaded Tresses Hat band is worked in seed stitch. You simply knit the hat-band (best done on a 40" needle, because of the smaller circumference, although it can be managed on a 47"), bind off half the stitches, then bring the bottom needle through the opening to meet the top needle so the remaining stitches can join in a simple circle, as shown next.

Turning a Moebius hat-band
into a simple circle

This Moebius hat-band has one half its stitches bound off. The remaining stitches are about to join in a simple circle. The lower needle will rise up to meet the upper needle.

The stitches are now lined up in a simple circle. But the needle is a little long, don't you think? Change to a 16" needle.

From here you knit upward, decreasing to form a bowl shape for the head. As you decrease away the stitches on your 16" needle, you'll have to

switch to a set of double-pointed needles, or work on two circular needles as shown to the right. You can use the 16" needle and the longer needle you used for the Moebius band, since length does not matter when knitting with two circular needles.

(I did not change to a 16" needle when taking the second photograph, but I hope you have!)

Knitting with Two Circular Needles

To knit with 2 circular needles, place half the stitches on each needle. Each needle ignores the other needle and knits its own stitches, then waits while the other needle knits its own stitches.

I am holding the ends of the working needle (which is in front). The other needle (which is in back) is snoozing with its stitches, as if it is a stitch holder.

Once the first needle finishes knitting its stitches, the yarn has moved into place for the second needle to use. When that needle finishes knitting its stitches, the first needle takes the yarn. And around and around they go, like a team of relay runners, handing off the baton to each other as they circle the track, only in this case they are handing the working yarn to each other.

Here I have knit halfway across the first needle. See the second needle sleeping below? When I finish knitting across the first needle, the second needle will wake up, take the yarn, and get to work, while the first needle sleeps. They keep taking turns working and sleeping.

If you have any trouble getting the tension right between the two needles, here is a solution: When you switch needles, knit your first stitch without worrying about the tension. Now insert your needle into the second stitch, and before actually knitting it, give the yarn a tug to snug up the first stitch. It will hold.

See the opposite side of the Reversible Lotus Hat on the next page

The two circular needle technique is also used in the Mischievous Feet chapter, and you may enjoy using this method for socks, hats, gloves, mittens, necks, and sleeves as well. For a more thorough discussion of knitting with two circular needles, please refer to my book, *Socks Soar on two Circular Needles.*

REVERSIBLE LOTUS BLOSSOM

This richly textured hat seems almost sculpted, although it truly is not difficult to make. It is completely reversible, with the design different on each side. Both designs have a lotus-like quality to them. The alpaca yarn comes from Honey Lane Farms on San Juan Island, Washington.

Materials: Honey Lane Farms Alpaca (100% Alpaca, 50 g/ 110 yds, 13 wpi) cinnamon or heathered lilac, 3 skeins

Needles: (you may require a different size to get correct gauge) circular size 9 (5.5 mm), 40" length, plus 16" circular or a set of double-pointed needles in same size

Notions: tapestry needle, 2 stitch markers in contrasting colors

Gauge: 13 sts = 4" (10 cm) with 2 strands of yarn held together, in slightly stretched stockinette

Finished size: adult - head circumference 20-23"

Stitch guide*: See page 111 for abbreviations. See page 60 for how to work with two circular needles. Use two strands held together throughout.

Beginning – Moebius hat-band
MCO 60. Place marker. Knit 3 rounds. Purl 3 rounds. Knit 3 rounds.

Finishing Moebius hat-band
Loosely bind off 60 sts, or use the elastic bind-off: Knit 2, * replace 2 sts on left needle and knit them together from right to left through back loops, k1, repeat from *. Bring needle ends together with band pushed below, so needle tips join in a simple circle as shown on page 60.

Begin crown
With 16" circular needle (or set of double-pointeds) and with 3 k rows facing you, p 1 round (use 16" needle to p sts from 40" needle, then put 40"

needle away). *Purl 1, p1f&b, repeat from * to marker (90 sts) Purl 1 round.

Crown grows upward

Round 1: *K1, p9, repeat from * to marker.

Round 2: *M1R, k1, M1L, p3, p3tog, p3, repeat from * to marker.

Round 3: *Knit 3, p7, repeat from * to marker.

Round 4: *Knit 1, M1R, k1, M1L, k1, p2, p3tog, p2, repeat from * to marker.

Round 5: *Knit 5, p5, repeat from * to marker.

Round 6: *Knit 2, M1R, k1, M1L, k2, p1, p3tog, p1, repeat from * to marker.

Round 7: *Knit 7, p3, repeat from * to marker.

Round 8: *Knit 3, M1R, k1, M1L, k3, p3tog, repeat from * to marker.

Round 9: *Knit 9, p1, repeat from * to marker, remove marker, p4, place marker here.

Repeat rounds 2-9.

Repeat rounds 2-5.

Crown decreases

Round 1: *Knit 5, p1, p3tog, p1, repeat from * to marker. (72 sts)

Round 2: *Knit 5, p3, repeat from * to marker.

Round 3: *Knit 5, p3tog, repeat from * to marker. (54 sts)

Rounds 4 - 7: *Knit 5, p1, repeat from * to marker. Repeat this round three times.

Round 8: *Knit 1, cdd, k1, p1, repeat from * to marker. (36 sts)

Rounds 9 - 11: *Knit 3, p1, repeat from * to marker. Repeat this round twice.

Round 12: *Cdd, p1, repeat from * to marker. (18 sts)

Rounds 13 – 14: *K 1, p1, repeat from * to marker. Repeat this round once.

Round 15: *Ssk, repeat from * to marker. (9 sts)

Finishing

Cut yarn and weave end through remaining 9 sts, pull snug and secure ends.

Yarn and design suggestions

Choose yarns soft against your skin and smooth enough to show off the sculptured stitches. Since variegated yarns often camouflage texture, look for something in one color. If you'd like to use a variegated yarn, you might use it just for the hat-band, and work the crown in one of the hat-band colors (Honey Lane Farms offers hand-painted colorways to match their single-color yarns, all in the same alpaca you see here). And your hat would still be reversible!

Jeweled Merino Cap

The crown of this cap begins differently than the previous one. After working applied I-cord all the way around the small Simplest-of-All Moebius Scarf that forms the hat-band, you pick up a crown-sized circle of stitches just beneath the I-cord edge and knit upward. The crown details are the result of a simple purl-3-together decrease. You'll find, once you put the cap on, that the rim can be worn either narrow or wide, because bipolar stockinette is happy to fold itself together, or stretch to warm your ears.

Materials: Louet Gems Merino sport weight (100% merino wool, 100 g/ 225 yds, 15 wpi), cherry red, charcoal, indigo, 1 skein each

Needles: (you may require a different size to get correct gauge) size 9 (5.5 mm) circular 40" or 47" length, plus 16" circular or set of double-pointed in same size

Notions: tapestry needle, stitch marker

Gauge: 16 sts = 4" (10 cm) with two strands held together, in slightly stretched stockinette

Size: adult - head circumference 20-23"

Stitch guide: See page 111 for abbreviations. Work with 2 strands of yarn held together throughout.

Hat-Band

With red, MCO 88. Place marker. Knit 5 rounds. Cut tail of red. With charcoal, work 3-st applied I-cord (see pages 28-29). Graft ends together.

Crown begins

With red, and 16" circular needle or double-pointed needles, pick up and k 88 sts between I-cord and reverse stockinette (purl side) beneath it. Join ends in a simple circle of 88 sts, as shown on page 60. Cut tail of red. Place marker.

Crown grows

Round 1: With indigo, knit.
Round 2: *Knit 7, k1f&b, repeat from * 10 times. (99 sts)

Rounds 3 – 10: Knit.

Round 11: *Knit 7, p2tog, place marker, repeat from * 10 times. There will already be a marker after last repeat. (88 sts)

Rounds 12 – 13: Knit.

Round 14: *Knit to 2 sts before next marker, p2tog, repeat from * 10 times. (77 sts)

Rounds 15 – 16: Knit.

Repeat rounds 14-16 until there are 22 sts left. Knit 2 rounds.

Close crown

Round 1: *Purl 2tog 11 times.

Round 2: Knit.

Round 3: Purl 2tog 4 times, p3tog.

Rounds 4-6: Purl. Cut yarn and thread through final sts, then weave in ends.

Yarn Suggestions

Gems Merino is springy, soft, and comes in jewel-tone colors so beautiful you will linger longer than usual trying to choose. If you substitute, look in your stash or local yarn shop for yarn to give you the same gauge (with a single strand, or two held together, as I did), and which feels soft against your skin. The hat could be done in a single color as well, or little short bits of colorful fringe might be attached to the p3tog decreases on the crown – or beads? You could also work this hat in two strands of yarn as I did, but with one strand of one color throughout, and three other colors taking turns joining it. Have a look at the Merging Stripes Scarf in chapter three to see how this technique shifts colors through the purl ridges.

Beaded Tresses Hat

This hat has a sort of Tibetan-Egyptian air about it. Put it on, and I guarantee you'll break into a grin. Swing your head side to side, and watch the beaded tresses fly out like one of those carnival rides — mad teacups or something? It's been a while! Although this hat brings out the kid in everyone, after the initial hilarity most people admire its elegance and style. Wear it to the opera! For more photos of the hat and its matching scarf, see pages 52-53.

Yarn: Skacel Incanto (35% cotton, 30% acrylic, 23% linen, 12% rayon, 50g/ 95m, 11 wpi), #01 sandstone, #02 coral, #03 lapis, 1 ball each

Needles: (you may require a different size to get correct gauge) size 6 (4 mm) circular 40" length, plus 16" circular or a set of double-pointed needles in same size

Notions: about 30 (only 15 actually used, but bead holes are irregular so you need extras) medium recycled glass beads, tapestry needle, stitch marker, crochet hook narrow enough to fit easily through hole of glass beads, with enough space to pull yarn through as well.

Gauge: 16 sts = 4" (10 cm) in seed stitch (see stitch guide below)

Finished Size: adult - head circumference 20-23"

Stitch Guide: See page 111 for abbreviations. For gauge swatch, cast on 22 sts. Row 1: Knit 1, p1 to end. Row 2: Purl 1, k1 to end. Repeat rows 1 and 2 until swatch is about 3" high, then take row measurement in middle.

Hat-band

With lapis, MCO 88. Place marker. *K1, p1, repeat from * to marker. M1L. * P1, k1, repeat from * until piece measures 2" wide. Cut tail of lapis. With coral, work applied I-cord around entire edge (see pages 28-29). Graft or sew beginning and end of I-cord together.

Begin crown

With coral, pick up 1 st in each of 88 I-cord sts where they meet seed st. Knit 88 picked-up sts, joining ends in simple circle (see page 60). Knit 4 rounds. *Knit 3, work 3 knitted-cast-on sts from next st (see page 28), then bind off 3 sts you just cast on, repeat from * to marker. Knit 6 rounds. (88 sts)

*Knit 6, k2tog, repeat from * 10 more times. (77 sts) Knit 3 rounds.

*Knit 5, k2tog, repeat from * 10 times. (66 sts) Knit 2 rounds.

*Knit 4, k2tog, repeat from * 10 more times. (55 sts) Knit 3 rounds.

*Knit 3, k2tog, repeat from * 10 more times. (44 sts) Knit 2 rounds.

*Knit 2, k2tog, repeat from * 10 more times. (33 sts) Knit 3 rounds.

*Knit 1, k2tog, repeat from * 10 more times. (22 sts) Knit 2 rounds.

*Knit 2tog 11 times. (11 sts)

Knit 1, k2tog, k4, k2tog, k2. Cut yarn and thread through final sts, then weave in ends.

Make and attach 15 beaded tresses

With sandstone and 16" circular or 1 double-pointed needle, cast on 3 sts, leaving 8" tail. Work free I-cord: *Slide 3 sts to top of needle, so working yarn comes from bottom of 3rd st. Knit 3. Repeat from * until 7" long. Cut 8" tail, use crochet hook to draw tail through 3 remaining sts. Use crochet hook to draw same tail through a bead, then through bottom of I-cord, through bead again, then weave tail up and down through center of I-cord. Attach beaded tresses: Use remaining tail to sew first beaded tress to inside of hat-band, 4" from center of twist. Sew second beaded tress 4" to other side of center. Sew remaining beaded tresses evenly distributed between the first two.

Yarn and design suggestions

The Incanto yarn which inspired this hat shimmers with glints of light. As you ponder other yarn choices, consider doing the hat in one variegated colorway with contrasting-colored beads – perhaps a lavender-hued colorway with snow white beads? Experiment! A winter version could be done in fine wool. The beaded tresses may also be knit shorter or longer, as you wish. You might also layer the tresses, make them a lot longer, then pull them into two braids. Have fun with your hand-knit hair!

In *The Second Treasury of Magical Knitting*, the techniques from this chapter evolve into felted bowls and feline bliss beds, like the one shown below. Here's Shey, a fine fellow from British Columbia, demonstrating correct paw placement (right on the Moebius twist).

Shey is having happy dreams in a feline bliss bed knit of Philosopher's Wool, ringed with Cat's Paw Fair Isle

Mischievous Feet

What has no inside or outside, only an upside and a downside, yet can safely hold your valuables?
The Magical Knitting Riddle

Chapter Eight– Mischievous Feet

I really couldn't write a knitting book without socks . . . and I hope these lighthearted versions will delight you as much as they do me.

If you've never knit socks before, perhaps this is the place to start. The felted boots will disguise any but the most grievous mistakes. And at the end of the chapter you'll find a playful sock necklace with particularly detailed instructions for knitting the seven socklings that dance around its single surface.

A Moebius scarf can turn into a pair of felted boots, believe it or not. The scarf becomes the handle (so you can pull yourself up by your Moebius bootstraps, should it ever become necessary) as well as the boot's rim – all it takes is a little bit of magic to open the space for your foot to step into.

To see how this works, make yourself a paper Moebius (see page 7). Now take your scissors and cut along the spine about one third of the way around. Pull the sides of the opening apart and peek through the eye-shaped opening. You are looking inside the boot you are about to make! Of course it is not there yet, but you can imagine it.

Basic process for knitting a Felted Moebius Boot

One: Knit small Moebius band with magic opening.
Two: Finish edge of Moebius band.
Three: Pick up stitches around magic opening for knitting boot on down to toe.
Four: Add fringe, and felt.

Now, there is something you need to know about these boots. You cannot put your foot inside them. You may think you can, but they have no inside, so you can't. Sorry.

The boot is nothing more than a "stretching" of the original Moebius band, as if it were made of a rubber sheet and a heavy foot stepped on the band, pressing out a boot shape.

This does not compromise our pure-hearted Moebius, which has but one edge and one surface (even if the illusion of duality persists).

If you follow the surface of the boot up the handle, you'll travel along that mysterious half twist, which will turn you over and drop you right down into what appears to be the inside of the boot. But how can it be the inside, when you can rise back up the "inside" wall to travel back over the handle's surface, which then pours you right back "outside?" There is no way to leave the single endless surface. You have been laboring under the illusion of duality too long.

This most mischievous footwear is remarkably practical as well. The Moebius handle is designed to be pushed behind the leg so the boots can be worn as cozy indoor boots, or if you slip a jar down the leg, they make splendid flower vases. Pour an inch of rice or beans into the boot to stabilize it, and you have a knitting needle holder, or a pencil container. I have an assortment of sizes and colors leaning amiably against each other in a corner and it looks like large elves live with me.

Fitting and felting guide for Moebius Boots

Please review the felting information on pages 37-38. Always examine your knitting before felting, and if there are any weak spots or holes, weave them up with a strand of the same yarn. No one will ever know you did this, because the stitches will melt into felted oblivion.

You must take special care when felting fringe, so you do not end up with thick clumps instead of charming spindly dreadlocks. Check the boots every one to two minutes for the first five minutes or so, to pull the fringe apart as it starts to clump. In my experience, most of the wayward socializing that goes on among fringe individuals happens in the first two minutes, and if you don't pull them apart then, it's too late. After you separate them the first time, they make fewer and fewer attempts to join in fibrous matrimony with their neighbors.

Once you have the rowdy fringes under control, let the boots agitate until the desired size is reached. It is ideal to shape the boot on the foot that will wear it, if it is to be worn. If it is to be a container or art object, or the foot in question is not nearby, place a plastic bag inside the boot and fill it with birdseed, beans, or rice, pressing and adjusting the boot so that it looks like a real foot.

Allow it to dry overnight with the bag of grain still inside, then in the morning tip the boot upside down into a bowl, remove the plastic bag, feed the birds, pat the boot back into shape, and let it finish drying where you can admire it.

The boot is given in three sizes, to fit a child five to eight years old, a woman, and a man, approximately. Measure the foot you wish to fit and use the size that matches it most closely (foot circumference is probably the most important measurement), then make adjustments as follows: To make the foot or leg longer, knit 1.5" more for

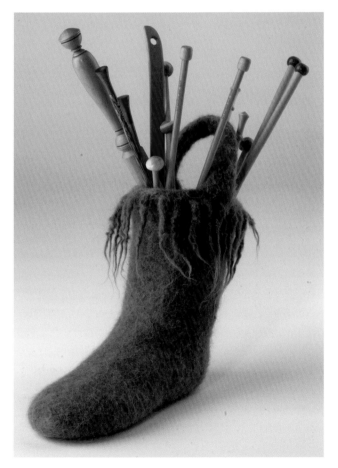

every 1" you wish to add to the felted version. To make the foot or leg shorter, knit 1.5" less for every 1" you wish to subtract from the felted version.

Plan to felt the boot about an inch longer than the foot it is to fit, for some wiggle room. During your frequent checks of the felting, you can choose to stop the shrinking process at any point within a several inch size range. If the width is still a bit big, but the length looks like it's going to be too small soon, tug the foot until the width narrows and the length is better. If you'd like the top of the boot to be larger, just give it a good tug and it will be. A freshly felted boot can usually be pushed and pulled to grow 1" to 2" in any direction, unless you have let it go too long. The final size is up to you.

I recommend that you do a test swatch with your yarn, if you have enough, by simply knitting a test boot which may or may not fit anyone. Use it as an art object, and once you are familiar with what your yarn does with your water in your washing machine, you will be able to make a boot to fit someone. You see, there are so many variables in felting, from hardness or softness of water to how the yarn was processed or dyed, that you are best off this way.

If you want to know if a yarn will felt, try this: cut a two inch piece and lay it in one palm. Dampen it (spit works) and then rub it between your palms fiercely for a minute like a boy scout trying to start a fire. Relax, and take a look. Is it felted? Then you have felting yarn. Is it just pathetic looking? You have yarn that is not going to felt. Use it for something else.

The Magic Opening – Waste yarn

You'll need this as soon as you have knit halfway around your first round.

The working yarn waits while the waste yarn knits a section of stitches. Slide the waste yarn stitches back to the left needle (not shown).

The working yarn knits right over the waste yarn stitches without treating them any differently than working stitches.

The waste yarn stitches are now safely sandwiched between two rows of working stitches.

Picking up waste yarn stitches

When you turn over the knitting to the waste yarn's purl side, you see each stitch held in a waste yarn loop. Pick up each stitch with

a needle. Many knitters find it easiest to do this with two needles, but it works just fine with one circular needle as well.

Felted Moebius Boots
Basic Version

Using Cascade 220 in #8895 red and #9332 blue

This is a detailed, instructional pattern, which I recommend you read through. I discuss special felting techniques and teach you to make the magical opening in the Moebius band. Make sure to read the felting and fitting instructions carefully, since felting has a magical life of its own. By the way, the boots you're about to knit answer the riddle at the start of this chapter.

Yarn: Feltable yarn (see page 71). If you want to use several colors, make them the same kind of yarn, to keep the felting even. Use 2 strands of a sport to light worsted yarn held together, or 1 strand of a heavy worsted weight yarn. You will also need less than 1 yard of smooth waste yarn in a contrasting color.

Needles: (you may require a different size to get correct gauge) size 11 (8mm) circular 40"– 55" length (use 40" length for size small), plus same size 16" length or a set of double-pointeds; a medium-sized crochet hook

Yardage requirements: (for two boots) 275 (400, 600) yds; double yardage if using two strands held together.

Notions: tapestry needle, stitch markers

Gauge: 13 sts = 4" (10 cm)

Unfinished, unfelted size: small – a child (medium – a woman, large – a man), length 9" (13", 17.5"), foot circumference 8" (11.5", 13.5"), height 9.5" (14", 17")

Finished, felted size: small – a child (medium – a woman, large – a man), length 7" (10", 12.5"), foot circumference 6" (8", 11")", height 7.5" (10", 12")

Stitch Guide: See page 111 for abbreviations.

Make the Moebius band, which becomes both handle and boot-rim

MCO 35 (45, 50). Place marker. Knit 57 (71, 77). Use waste yarn to knit next 13 (19, 23) sts. Slide the 13 (19, 23) waste yarn sts back on to left needle. Now knit back across those 13 (19, 23) waste yarn sts using regular yarn (see page 72). Purl 1 round.

Finish edge with applied I-cord (see pages 28-29), and graft or sew ends together. You have completed handle and boot-rim.

Open the waste yarn section to begin boot

Use 16" circular needle (or 2 circular needles) to pick up (but not knit) the 26 (38, 46) sts waste yarn is holding (see page 72). Remove the waste yarn. Pick up 1 additional st in each intersection, so that you have a leg of 28 (40, 48) sts.

Leg

Knit around on 28 (40, 48) sts until leg is 5.5" (7.5", 10") long.

Heel Flap

The heel flap is a square which is knit on half the leg stitches. It covers the back of your heel.

Place next 14 (20, 24) sts on a holder, and work remaining sts back and forth to make a square heel flap.

Row 1: Turn and sl 1 pwise, p until 1 st is left, k1.

Row 2: Turn, sl 1 pwise, k to end.

Repeat rows one and two 6 (9, 11) more times.

Turn the heel

At the base of the heel flap you work short rows to make a small cup shape.

Row 1: (start on wrong side) Purl 9 (12, 14), ssp, p1, turn.

Row 2: Slip 1 kwise, k5, k2tog, k1, turn.

Row 3: Slip 1 pwise, p to 1 st before gap, ssp (1 st from either side of gap), p1, turn.

Row 4: Slip 1 kwise, k to 1 st before gap, k2tog (1 st from either side of gap), k1, turn.

Repeat rows 3 and 4 until you reach the end of a purl row and no st remains after the ssp. Turn.

Final row: Slip 1 kwise, k until 2 sts left, k2tog.

Pick up gusset stitches

You pick up stitches in the long loops along the sides of the heel flap.

Pick up and knit 7 (10, 12) in loops along left side of heel flap, pu and k1 in between heel flap and instep (top of foot), k1 from holder, place marker, k until 1 st remains on holder, place marker, k1, discard holder, pu and k1 just before heel flap, pu and k7 (10, 12) in loops along right side of heel flap, and k to 2 sts before first marker. *Note: When you have too few sts to spread easily around your 16" needle, place one set of between-the-marker stitches on a second circular needle and leave the other set on your 16" needle (you may use 2 lengths, like the 40" or 47" and 16" you already have). See instructions on page 60 for knitting with 2 circular needles.*

Work the gusset

By working regular decreases beginning near top of both sides of heel flap, you create triangular gussets to fit the downward slope of your foot.

Round 1: Knit tog the 2 sts before first marker, k to second marker, ssk, k to first marker.

Round 2: Knit until 2 sts before first marker.

Repeat rounds 1 and 2 until 24 (36, 42) sts remain.

Foot

Knit all sts evenly until foot is 7" (10.5", 14") long. To measure, fold sock flat (like a sideways foot) and measure from fold at back of heel to needle. Place each set of 12 (18, 21) sts between markers on a separate circular needle, if they are not already on one.

Toe

Round 1: *Knit 1, ssk, k to 3 sts from end of needle, k2tog, k1, repeat from * on second needle.

Round 2: Knit 1round.

Repeat rounds 1 and 2 until 8 (12, 13) sts remain on each needle.

Repeat round 1 until 4 (6, 9) sts remain on each needle.

Graft the 2 sets of 4 (6, 9) sts together (see I-cord grafting on page 29). You may also bind them off and sew them together. After felting, no one will ever really know how you finished the toe.

Fringe and felt

Cut about 28 five-inch (45 eight-inch, 48 eight-inch) lengths of yarn, fold them in half, and pull them through each st of lower edge of I-cord with crochet hook, and pull ends snug through fringe loop. Felt according to directions at start of this pattern.

Sophie's Mermaid Feet

I think these boots would look so natural on a mermaid, with their undersea colors and seaweedy fringe. The first pair of felted Moebius boots I made, they are utterly enchanting. Right now I have one on my table holding a bouquet of yellow tulips streaked in pink. The exquisite, hand-painted yarn comes from two magical women in Pennsylvannia, who offer this particular yarn only in "Lottery" colorways, allowing themselves to create new color combinations at whim. But I suspect they'd be willing to make more of something similar to this colorway if enough yarn shops ask for it.

Yarn: Wool in the Woods Sophie (50% wool, 50% llama, 200 yards, 9 wpi), 2 skeins for small and medium, 3 skeins for large, in Lottery colorway dark brown, olive, mummy, dark green, bright green. Less than 1 yard smooth waste yarn in a contrasting color.

FOLLOW THE FELTED MOEBIUS BOOTS, BASIC VERSION ON PAGE 72, AND MAKE THE SIZE YOU WISH. BOOTS SHOWN ARE SIZE MEDIUM.

ENCHANTED FOREST
CHRISTMAS STOCKING

The tree growing out of the side of this holiday boot is lush and wild. Like a real tree, it has thick boughs which a small creature might burrow into. Your children will love digging their fingers into the cushy felted foilage, which is added before felting the boot (I've been asked this question often, so there's your answer). You could add colored beads to the tree, or even trim the tree with tiny beaded ornaments that could be added to and rearranged every year, starting a family tradition.

Yarn: Crystal Palace Iceland (100% wool, 109 yds/ 100 g, 8 wpi), #8166 red, 2 balls, #4043 evergreen, 1 ball; Crystal Palace Fizz (100% polyester, 120 yds/ 50 g, 15 wpi) #9154 sage, 1 ball. This will make one boot. For two boots, you need 4 balls red, but just 1 evergreen and sage. Find a small amount of brown feltable yarn for the trunk. You also need about 1 yard smooth waste yarn in a contrasting color.

Needles: (you may require a different size to get correct gauge) size 11 (8 mm) circular 40" - 55" length, size 11 (8 mm) circular 16" length or set of double-pointed needles; medium crochet hook

Notions: tapestry needle, stitch markers

Gauge: 12 sts = 4" (10 cm)

Unfelted Size: foot length 14.5", cuff circumference 15", height 16", handle 10" long and 2" wide.

Felted (finished) Size: foot length 10.5", cuff circumference 12", height 11", handle 8" long and 1.25" wide.

Stitch Guide: see page 111 for abbreviations.

FOLLOW THE FELTED MOEBIUS BOOTS, BASIC VERSION ON PAGE 72, IN SIZE LARGE, WITH THE FOLLOWING CHANGES:

Moebius band
Use red yarn until ready to work I-cord. Cut tail of red. Use green yarn to work applied I-cord.

Leg
With red, knit until 10" long.

Foot
Knit until foot is 14" long.

ADD TREE DESIGN

Cut 5" lengths of Fizz and Iceland, and use 1 strand of each for each fringe piece. Cut about 35 fringe pairs to start and add more as needed. Top of tree starts 1.5" beneath rim, centered under handle, and is 6" tall and 3.5" wide at base. The trunk, which is loosely embroidered with brown yarn, is 2" wide at base and tapers to 1" where it meets greenery. The trunk begins about half an inch beneath top of gusset triangle.

To attach fringe, fold in half and use crochet hook to pull loop end through horizontal strands that run between sts, then pull ends through loop and tug snugly. Place fringe 2 sts apart and 2 rows apart, staggering placement row to row. The easiest way to embroider the trunk is to loosely wrap each column of sts with brown yarn, using a tapestry needle. Make sure to follow fringe felting directions carefully as given on page 70.

Buckskin Boot

The yarn I used for this boot is dyed just unevenly enough to give a buckskin appearance, perfect for a youngster who loves to dress up and play in the world of the imagination. Every yarn felts a little differently, offering you its own surprises, as you will see when you experiment.

Yarn: Araucania (100% wool, 100g/ 242 yds, 15 wpi), 3 skeins, small amount waste yarn

Needles: Size 11 (8 mm) circular 40 or 47" (100 or 120 cm) length, size 11 (8 mm) circular 16" (40 cm) length or set of double-pointed needles; medium crochet hook

Notions: tapestry needle, stitch markers

Gauge: 12 sts = 4" (10 cm)

Unfelted Size: Foot length 14.5", cuff circumference 15", height 16"

Felted (finished) Size: Foot length 9.5", cuff circumference 12", height 11"

Stitch Guide: See page 111 for abbreviations.

FOLLOW FELTED MOEBIUS BOOTS, BASIC VERSION ON PAGE 72, IN SIZE MEDIUM.

CHILD'S WOODLAND BOOTS

Can't you see a little child scampering through a meadow wearing these? The bouquet in this boot and the Buckskin Boot came from Nootka Rose Farm on one of the "outer islands" of the San Juan Island archipelago, where children do scamper through the woods in glorious freedom, and have eyes that shine like a fawn's.

Yarn: Cascade 220 (100% wool, 100g/ 220 yds, 11 wpi), forest #9435, 1 skein; meadow #7814, 1 skein for 1 boot and 2 skeins for 2 boots

FOLLOW FELTED MOEBIUS BOOTS, BASIC VERSION, PAGE 72, IN SIZE SMALL, USING TWO STRANDS OF YARN HELD TOGETHER, WITH THE —FOLLOWING CHANGES:

Moebius band
Use meadow until ready to work I-cord. Cut tail of meadow. Use forest to work applied I-cord.

Leg
Use meadow.

Fringe
Use forest for fringe.

SEVEN SOCKLINGS NECKLACE

It seems like there ought to be a fairy tale about the Moebius necklace of the seven socklings! I finished the prototype just in time for Stitches West. I had it on my head like a wreath until Ann Bourgeois of Philosopher's Wool graciously hinted I might like to wear it as a necklace instead. Either way, you'll turn heads and gather smiles. An elementary school teacher could wear it every day; the rest of us will have to be more patient.

I must point out that the necklace, like Moebius boots, has no inside or outside. The socklings are simply extensions, or stretchings, of the Moebius they grow from. Yet, magically, even without an inside or outside, you may safely store your jewels, keys, or grocery list in them, and they will stay put unless you turn the Moebius sockling itself upside down. You see, we have no inside or outside, but we do have an upside and downside, and of course, a oneside. Such are the marvels of Moebius knitting.

Yarn: Get out your stash of left over mini-balls of sock yarn. You will need a small amount of one color for the Moebius "scarf" which serves as the necklace "chain", and a small amount of sock yarn for each of the 7 socklings. You'll also need about 2 yards waste yarn.

Needles: 40" circular in size to suit your yarns, and a pair of circulars or set of double-pointeds for knitting the sockling siblings.

Notions: Use any notions that come into your head to fancy up this playful sockling Moebius. You'll also want a tapestry needle and a stitch marker.

Gauge: Something sock-like.

My gauge is 26 sts = 4" (10 cm).

Finished size: This depends on all your previous answers! Mine is 26" circumference and the socklings are about 3" high.

Stitch Guide: See page 111 for abbreviations.

Note: Pattern is written for 2 circular needles.

Begin necklace-band

With necklace color and 40" needle, MCO 154. Place marker.

Round 1: Knit 154. (See page 72 for waste yarn instructions.) *Knit 11 sts with waste yarn. Cut tail of waste yarn. Replace sts on left needle and knit over waste yarn with regular yarn. Knit 11 sts. Repeat from * 6 times.

Rounds 2-3: Knit.

Rounds 4-6: Purl.

Bind off loosely.

Knit the seven socklings

Use a separate circular needle to pick up each set of 11 waste yarn sts (see page 72 for waste yarn instructions, and page 60 for how to knit with 2 circulars). Choose one of the seven sockling yarns and *k 11, pick up and k 1 in the intersection, repeat from * once. (24 sts) Knit all rounds for about 2", then rearrange sts so that each needle moves forward 6 sts (to do this, knit 6 sts from next needle, then rearrange sts evenly on needles.)

Heel Flap

Leave 12 stitches to rest on one needle while you work back and forth on the other:

Row 1: Knit 12.

Row 2: Slip 1 pwise, p10, k1.

Row 3: Slip 1 pwise, k11. Repeat rows 2 and 3 until you have a total of 12 rows on heel flap.

Turn heel

Row 1: Slip 1 pwise, k6, k2tog, k1, turn.

Row 2: Slip 1 pwise, p3, ssp, p1, turn.

Row 3: Slip 1 pwise, k4, k2tog, k1, turn.

Row 4: Slip 1 pwise, p5, ssp, p1, turn.

Row 5: Slip 1 pwise, k7.

Pick up gusset stitches

With same needle you've been using, pick up and k 6 sts in loops along heel flap, and pick up and k 1 st in corner between heel flap instep (top of foot) needle. Knit 6 instep sts from other needle. Now let working needle rest, while you use both ends of other needle to knit next 6 instep sts, pick up and k 1 st in corner between instep needle and heel flap, and pick up and k 6 sts in loops along this side of heel flap. Knit 4 of the heel turn sts from other needle. You now have 17 stitches on each needle, and the little sock is in profile.

Work the gusset

Knit one round:

First needle: Knit 4 (heel turn sts), knit 7 (picked up sts) tbl, k 6 (instep sts). Second needle: Knit 6 (instep sts), k7 (picked up sts) tbl, knit 4 (heel turn sts).

Now you will decrease every other round

Round 1: Knit 9, k2tog, k12, ssk, k9.
Round 2: Knit 32.
Round 3: Knit 8, k2tog, k12, ssk, k8.
Round 4: Knit 30.
Round 5: Knit 7, k2tog, k12, ssk, k7.
Round 6: Knit 28
Round 7: Knit 6, k2tog, k12, ssk, k6.
Round 8: Knit 26
Round 9: Knit 5, k2tog, knit 12, ssk, k5.
Round 10: Knit 24
Round 11: Knit 4, k2tog, k12, ssk, k4.
Round 12: Knit 22

Foot

Continue knitting rounds of 22 stitches until foot is 3/4" shorter than desired.

Toe

Round 1: Knit 4, cdd, k8, cdd, k4.
Round 2: Knit 18.
Round 3: Knit 3, cdd, k6, cdd, k3.
Round 4: Knit 14.
Round 5: Knit 2, cdd, k4, cdd, k2.
Round 6: Knit 10.

Knit 3 more sts onto needle you just finished with. Then pick up next needle and knit its 2 stitches plus 3 from other needle. Your sock is now lying face-front, ready to be grafted. Graft (see page 29) or sew toe, weave in ends, and make next sockling same way, until you have completed all seven.

Moss Felted Basket

A look into

The Second Treasury of Magical Knitting

all Moebius in nature, with no inside or outside. But don't worry . . . they can safely hold your valuables. Here are a few inside-less and outside-less designs to ponder . . .

Jester Tentacle bags

Felted Foursome Basket

Fanny Basket

Fringed Bowl

Cat Bliss Bed with Paws & Tail

Every time I wear my Lost Trail Cape, I'm surrounded again by the effortlessness and powerful grace that was present at the weekend workshop. Magical Knitting Workshop student, Vancouver, British Columbia

CHAPTER NINE – SWIRLING CAPES

H ere are two unusual capes for you to wrap yourself in. Both begin as a Moebius scarf, which is partially bound off, reserving enough edge stitches to begin knitting the capes from the top down. The Rimrock Cape drops over your head and is wonderfully elastic so you can move about within its warm cocoon. Its diagonally-patterned Moebius collar-scarf hangs gracefully in layers of textured yarn. The Lost Trail Cape opens down the front, and has a wondrous Moebius scarf which can be worn as a hood, a double neck wrap, a long scarf, or folded back to become a wide collar.

Both Moebius scarves have special patterning, and you may choose to knit the scarves alone, working the edgings all the way around instead of saving some stitches for beginning the cape. At the end of a workshop I gave for the West Coast Knitters' Guild in British Columbia, Lynne Anderson of Knitopia (in White Rock, British Columbia) brought in an enormous basket of hand-painted yarns from Fleece Artist in Nova Scotia. There was a small riot as knitters reached for what looked like huge, high-fiber, braided loaves of bread, but were actually three or four different textures of yarn dyed in one colorway, plaited together. I later learned that most of them were to become one of these capes.

RIMROCK CAPE

The Rimrock Cape was my first, and a vision of it incubated in my head for several months before I found just the right yarn. Mountain Colors Mohair and Moguls are a delicious combination when knit together on large needles, two rows of each alternating. The Mohair surrounds the lustrous, bumpy Moguls and allows its curled knots to shine, and the two together make a surprisingly elastic fabric so that your arms can do what they want. In fact, it's a bit chilly this morning, and I am wearing it as I type. The center of the cape's scarf is knit in Merino

Ribbon, sending a never-ending Moebius flow of this soft yarn around your neck. The neck opening is deep, and the scarf is wide, so if you would like to close the neck a little, find one beautiful button to sew on one side, and add a button loop on the other.

Yarn: 1 skein Mountain Colors Merino Ribbon (80% Super Fine Merino Wool, 20% nylon, 100g/ 245 yds, 10 wpi); 3 skeins Mountain Colors Moguls (98% wool, 2% nylon, 100g/ 65 yds, 4.25 wpi); 1 skein Mountain Colors Mohair (78% mohair, 13% wool, 9% nylon, 100g/ 225 yds, 8 wpi); all in Rimrock colorway.

Gauge: Merino Ribbon - 14 sts = 4" (10 cm) on size 10 needle; Moguls - 9 sts = 4" on size 13 needle.

Needles: (you may require a different size to get correct gauge) size 13 (9 mm) circular 47"– 60" length, size 10 (6 mm) circular 47"– 60" length

Notions: tapestry needle, 2 stitch markers in contrasting colors

Finished Size: Moebius collar is 42" circumference, 12" wide at neckline and 14" wide at bottom of front opening, cape is 26" from back neckline to hem.

Stitch Guide: See page 111 for abbreviations.

Moebius Collar

With merino ribbon and size 10 needle, MCO 130. Place marker. Knit 1 round, p 1 round.

Begin diagonal pattern

Round 1: *K5, p5, repeat from * to end of round.

Round 2 and all even-numbered rounds: repeat previous round.

Round 3: Purl 1, *k5, p5, repeat from * to end, finishing with p4.

Round 5: Purl 2, *k5, p5, repeat from * to end, finishing with p3.

Round 7: Purl 3, *k5, p5, repeat from * to end, finishing with p2.

Round 9: Purl 4, *k5, p5, repeat from * to end, finishing with p1.

Round 11: *Purl 5, k5, repeat from * to end.

Round 13: Knit 1, *p5, k5, repeat from * to end, finishing with k4.

Round 15: Knit 2, *p5, k5, repeat from * to end, finishing with k3.

Round 17: Knit 3, *p5, k5, repeat from * to end, finishing with k2.

Round 19: Knit 4, *p5, k5, repeat from * to end, finishing with k1.

Rounds 20-21: Repeat rounds 1- 2. Cut tail of Merino Ribbon.

This completes Merino Ribbon part of collar. Now you work a 2-row Mohair edging on the part of collar that will hang free, leaving 85 sts unworked. The 85 sts become the foundation of the cape, which will grow out of them.

Row 1: With Mohair, *k5, p5 repeat from *, end k5, until 85 sts remain. Turn work around.

Row 2: *Purl 5, k5 repeat from * to 5 sts before marker, p5. Turn work around. (85 sts remain unworked).

Bind off 175 sts, leaving 85 sts on needle.

Begin cape

With Mohair and size 13 needle, working on remaining 85 sts, k22, place first marker, k41, place second marker, k22. Cut tail of Mohair. With knit side facing you, slide first 22 sts to right needle tip so you can begin knitting at first marker. Resume knitting with Mohair.

Row 1: Knit 42 (1 st past second marker), turn work. Without cutting Mohair, begin with Moguls. Work next 2 rows with Moguls alone. From now on, switch between Mohair and Moguls every 2 rows or rounds. Take care to twist yarns loosely around one other each time they pass on wrong side of cape.

Row 2: Slip 1, p42 (1 st past first marker), turn work.

Row 3: Slip 1, k43 (2 sts past second marker), turn work.

Row 4: Slip 1, p44 (2 sts past first marker), turn work.

Repeat rows 3 and 4, knitting or purling 1 more st past marker each time, until you have knit or purled 22 sts past each marker, finally working all 85 sts left from Moebius collar. Remove markers. Use knitted cast-on (see page 28) to add 5 sts for a total of 90 sts on needle. Slide 5 new sts to left needle. Place marker and join ends, now knitting in a circle. *Knit 5, k1f&b, repeat from * to marker. You have 105 sts. Knit 14 rounds.

Increase round: *Knit 9, k1f&b, repeat from * to end of round, ending k5. (115 sts) Knit 14 rounds.

Increase round: *Knit 10, k1f&b, repeat from * to end of round, ending k5. (125 sts) Knit 14 rounds. Cut tail of Moguls.

Holding a strand of Merino Ribbon and one of Mohair together, *k24, k1f&b, repeat from * to end of round. Cut tail of Mohair and with Merino Ribbon alone, k5, p5 around for 3 rounds. Bind off *very* loosely.

Finishing collar

With Moguls and size 13 (9mm) needle, pick up and k 103 sts evenly distributed along the bound-off edge of the Moebius collar. Turn and k103. Drop Moguls, and with Mohair, k 4 rows. Drop Mohair and k 2 rows with Moguls. Repeat last 6 rows, then repeat last 2 rows. Cut tail of Moguls and use Mohair to loosely bind off. Sew ends of Mohair-Moguls border to 5 cast-on sts at the front of cape so that borders meet in middle, and to stabilize this area. Weave in loose ends.

Yarn and design suggestions

The springy, elastic nature of the loosely knit rows of Mohair and Moguls make this relatively close-fitting cape very functional. If you substitute with another yarn, knit a large swatch to make sure the fabric is similarly flexible. it would be interesting to use a second color to edge the scarf-collar and the hem.

Lost Trail Cape

Here we have a Moebius-collared cape with an opening down the front. The scarf-collar is attached only at the back of the neck, and this frees it to do everything a Moebius scarf can do, and more. It can swing low, falling into curves, or be wrapped twice around your neck, or once around your neck and over your head like a hood, or be folded back, with the twist behind you, like a collar. Little Red Riding Hood never had it this good!

Scarf worn as hood with neck-wrap

Yarn: Mountain Colors Moguls (98% wool, 2% nylon, 100g/ 65 yds, 4.25 wpi), 5 skeins; Mountain Colors Mohair (78% mohair, 13% wool, 9% nylon, 100g/ 225 yds, 8 wpi), 2 skeins; Mountain Colors Mountain Goat (55% mohair, 45% wool, 100g/ 230 yds, 12 wpi), 2 skeins, all in Lost Trail colorway.

Needles: (you may require a different size to get correct gauge) size 11 (8mm) and size 7 (4.5mm) circulars, 47" - 60" length

Notions: tapestry needle, stitch markers, 3 pewter clasps (mine are from Russi; see page 110)

Gauge: With Mountain Goat - 20 sts = 4"
(10 cm) on size 7 needle; Mohair or Moguls -
12 sts = 4" (10 cm) on size 11 needle

Stitch Guide: See page 111 for abbreviations.

Begin cape collar

MCO 240 sts with Moguls and size 7 needle. Cut
tail of Moguls to weave in later, place marker.

Establish k1p1 ribbing

With Mountain Goat, *k1, p1, repeat from * to
marker. Work 6 rounds ribbing.

Scarf worn long

Continuing with collar

*Drop Mountain Goat (but do not cut it).
With Moguls, work 1 round ribbing. Cut tail of
Moguls to weave in later. With Mountain Goat,
work 6 rounds ribbing. Repeat from * once.

Edge of collar

With Mountain Goat, work applied I-cord (see
pages 28-29) until only 51 collar sts remain on
left needle. Place the three I-cord sts on a holder.

Begin cape

*You will work 2 rows Mohair, then 2 rows of
Moguls throughout. Work rows 1 and 2 with
Mohair, work rows 3 and 4 with Moguls, and so
on. On the edge where the yarns take turns, twist the
strands around one another as they trade places,
and make sure they are loose enough for both sides
of front opening to hang evenly.*

Pick up neck stitches from collar, beginning
where I-cord sts are on holder
(leave I-cord on holder):

Row 1: Starting with Mohair and size 11 needle,
knit remaining 51 collar sts as follows: *Knit
2tog twice, k1, repeat from * twice, k2tog.
Repeat from * twice. Thirty sts remain on the
size 11 needle. Put away size 7 needle, which was
holding collar sts.

Row 2 and all even rows: Slip first st, p until
1 st remains, k1.

Begin increases for shoulders and neck

*A reminder: You've worked two rows,
so switch to Moguls now.*

Row 3: Slip first st, k1, k1 tbl in strand between
last st and next st,* k3, k1 tbl in strand between
sts, repeat from * 7 times, k3, k1tbl in strand
between sts, k1. (40 sts)

Row 5: (*Mohair*) Slip first st, k1, k1 tbl in strand

between last st and next st, work 8 increases spread out between here and last 2 sts on this row, k1 tbl in strand between last st and next st, k2. (50 sts)

Row 7: (*Moguls*) Slip first st, k1, k1tbl in strand between last st and next st, work 8 increases spread out between here and last 2 sts on this row, k1 tbl in strand between last st and next st, k1. (60 sts)

Row 9: (*Mohair*) Use knitted cast-on to make 5 more sts from first st on left needle. Knit to last st on needle and use knitted cast-on to make 5 more sts from this last st, remove them from left needle and replace them on right needle in proper sequence. (70 sts)

Continue regular increases

Row 11: (*Moguls*) To bring Moguls into working position, move first 6 sts from left needle to right needle, weaving Moguls in between sts as you replace them, one by one, onto left needle. Now begin knitting: Slip first st, k1, work 8 increases spread out between here and last 2 sts on this row, k2. (78 sts)

Row 13: (*Mohair*) Slip first st, k1, work 8 increases spread out between here and the last 2 sts on this row, k2. (86 sts)

Repeat rows 11-14 four times (150 sts).

Begin to increase less frequently

Work increase row (as in row 13) every 8 rows instead of every 2 rows, until you have 198 sts. Continue knitting on 198 sts until cape measures 18.5" from collar base. Decrease at end of each right side row as follows: Slip 1, ssk, k until 3 sts left, k2tog, k1. Continue working even rows as before. When 178 sts remain, complete wrong side row and set cape aside while you work facings for front opening. You will be needing this

long needle to work the applied I-cord edging, so you may want to place the 178 hem sts on another long circular needle or on a piece of string until you are ready to work them.

Scarf folded back as collar

Front facings

The cape requires facings to neutralize the tendency of stockinette fabric to curl inward. With Mohair and size 11 needle, cast on 7 sts and k all rows for 18.5". Identify this side of work with safety pin and begin to work short rows to match curve of hem corner: Knit 6, turn, slip 1, k to end. Knit 5, turn, slip 1, k to end. Knit 4, turn, slip 1, k to end. Turn, k7, and resume knitting all rows until strip just touches waiting hem sts with one corner. If necessary, knit one more row so that safety pin is on opposite side.

Now work short rows so facing shape matches botom curve of hem: Knit 6, turn, slip 1, k to end. Knit 5, turn, slip 1, k to end. Knit 4, turn, slip 1, k to end. Knit 3, turn, slip 1, k to end. Knit 2, turn, slip 1, k to end. Bind off. Make second facing just like this one for other side. Use strand of Mohair to loosely sew each facing strip to an inside edge, matching angles near hem.

Set up for applied I-cord hem

Working with size 11 needle and strand of Mountain Goat held together with strand of Mohair, pick up and k10 sts along left neck, starting from collar attachment. Turn and k10, turn and k10 again. Continuing down, pick up and knit 72 sts from the top left front down to the sts waiting on needle at hem. Knit across 178 sts at bottom hem of cape, then pick up and knit 72 sts along right front up to top corner, then 10 more along neck edge. Turn and k10, turn and k10 again. Turn around. You have 342 sts on the needle.

Applied I-cord hem

Three I-cord collar sts wait on a holder. Slip these sts onto left needle tip, and begin working applied I-cord with them(see pages 28-29). At the tip of each neck corner, work 2 rounds of I-cord without attaching it (*k all 3 sts, replace sts on left needle, repeat from * once), then resume working applied I-cord. When you reach last st on left side, weave remaining 3 sts together with beginning of collar I-cord (see page 29).

Finishing

Knit an I-cord length in Mountain Goat on size 7 needles, which when stretched, matches measurement of back of wearer's neck from one normal shoulder seam to the other. Cut 24" tail of yarn, and use it to sew I-cord on outside, along neckline between scarf and body of cape. Stretch the I-cord while sewing it, and weave ends securely to I-cord edge on either side. Sew the 3 pewter clasps to front, the first one at the top of neck, and next two 6" apart.

Yarn and design suggestions

If you would like to design your own Moebius cape, you'll find it easy after reading through these patterns. You simply marry a Moebius scarf with the neckline of a cape, taking into account how the scarf will fall from the neckline. Of course, you could also knit a cape and make a separate, matching Moebius scarf . . . but there is something magical about making one organic garment.

An especially enticing combination would be to complete a shaped scarf, like those in Chapter Four, then play with it in front of a mirror to choose a favorite mercurial drape around your shoulders, and design a cape growing out of the edges, or from beneath (just pick up stitches) so that the scarf lies over the cape with a collar effect. Perhaps you've already finished a shaped scarf and are halfway there! Need I say that the possibilities of both knitting and Moebii are endless?

Scarf wrapped twice around neck

My whole take on knitting is completely transformed.
I don't usually think of it as being this creative and playful.
West Coast Knitters Guild member, Vancouver, British Columbia

Chapter Ten – Undulating Adventures

This chapter welcomes the kind of knitter who might go bungee jumping in her spare time. It contains two beautiful scarves which can never be reproduced – any more than a stream of water can hold the same rivulets and waves twice. But you will learn to swim, I mean knit, your own Moebius stream, and it is remarkably easy.

These scarves are not designed to be knit by the perfectionist, unless you are a liberated perfectionist who knows that the most exquisite beauty comes from allowing nature to take its course.

I am not going to give you stitch by stitch instructions, because to do so would be not only laborious for both of us, but the result would be static instead of as exuberant and alive as a raven playing in billows of invisible air.

The scarves in this chapter are knit using a series of shortening and lengthening rows. I will teach you the technique of building swells and crossing narrows, and then abandon you to knit your own unique sequence of stream-like shapes as you slowly work your way back and forth, yet around and around, the Moebius spine of your own one-of-a-kind scarf.

SKY BLUE WIND SCARF

I'm not going to hold your hand as you knit this scarf, because that would make it hard for you to knit, and anyway . . . you are a liberated knitter! By the way, this yarn is so soft and luscious that you may want to just hold it for a day or two even before winding it into a ball. It is also a wonderful felting yarn. I love the way this scarf narrows and swells along the edges, just like water finding its way along a dry path. You'll find that these undulating edges explore the shapes of your neck, and then settle into place, if you just help them along by slowly rotating it around your neck in front of a mirror.

Yarn: Cascade Pastaza (50% llama, 50% wool, 100g/ 132 yds, 11 wpi), # 085 sky blue, 2 skeins.
Needles*: (you may require a different size to get correct gauge) size 10 (6 mm) circular 47"- 60" length
Gauge: 15 sts = 4" (10 cm)
Finished size: 36" circumference, width varies from 5"– 9"
Stitch Guide: See page 111 for abbreviations.

Beginning
MCO 135. Place marker.
Middle
Round 1: Knit.
Round 2: Purl.
Round 3: Sl&w 1 and turn. Place marker on left side of wrapped st.
Short row undulations
Knit 13, sl&w 1 and turn.
Knit 12, sl&w 1 and turn.
Knit 11, sl&w 1 and turn.

Continue in this pattern until you have perhaps 4-5 sts left. On a row where you are headed back towards marker, knit all the way to marker, then turn, and k all the way to the end of 13 sts. Repeat this process, on any number of sts (vary number from about 7 - 19), but rather than knit all the way back to marker, k either to beginning of previous undulation or a little way into it.

Undulation variations

Rather than shorten rows by 1 st, shorten them by 2 or 3 sts at one end and 1 st at the other; or any combination you like. You can also knit across several wrapped sts and then slip and wrap a wrapped st again, and turn around and come back to make a more pointed peak.

Work short row undulations all the way around and as you move to the second half of this round, try to make the undulations flow well with the ones they border by filling the concave dips. Be irregular, like water.

Finishing

When the scarf is about 5" - 8" wide all around (it will be irregular), begin edge: Knit 1round, p 1 round, bind off. You may want to pick up and bind off a few extra sts on hilltops of curves so they will expand well. Weave in ends.

Yarn and design suggestions

I hope you'll try this scarf in a hand-painted yarn as well. If you work in a much smaller gauge, you'll need to cast on more stitches of course, and you'll also find that as the size of the undulations diminishes, their visual impact will recede. It would be interesting to knit beads into some of the curves, spontaneously, of course.

Undulating Autumn Scarf

This design of this scarf was already very much alive in my mind, impatiently waiting its turn to be born. Then I unwrapped a gift from Sivia Harding, a dear friend and wonderful fiber artist, found a thick skein of her hand-painted yarn, and recognized it as the yarn I had been dreaming of. You cannot make the scarf you see in the picture, but don't fret. Seek out a yarn that has three to five colors repeating around the skein, or hand-paint your own. I give you the yarn weight and gauge I used, should you wish to approximate it, but the truth is that this scarf and the earlier one can be knit in any yarn at any gauge. Undulating Magical Knitting knows no bounds.

Yarn: Sivia Harding Hand-Paint (100% Lopi-like wool, 100g/ 110 yds, 6.5 wpi), blue-plum-loden-rust colorway, 2 skeins

Needles: (you may require a different size to get correct gauge) size 13 (9 mm) circular 47" - 60" length

Notions: tapestry needle, stitch markers

Gauge: 13 sts = 4" (10 cm)

Finished size as shown: circumference 48", width varies from 6"– 11"

Stitch Guide: *See page 111 for abbreviations. The MCO is worked in segments, with each segment knit back and forth in shortening, then lengthening rows, before casting on for the next one. When the line of swelling segments is long enough to suit a scarf, they practically ask to be joined, and you have to say yes. After a few rounds of "normal" knitting, continue to work shortening and lengthening segments into the spots calling for them. Do not fear, but pick up your needles and yarn and read on.*

Beginning

MCO 13. Do not join; simply turn work and begin with row 1 below.

Knit first ripple

Row 1: Knit 13, turn.

Row 2: Slip 1 pwise, k11, sl&w 1, turn.

Row 3: Slip 1 pwise, k 1 st fewer than the last row, sl&w 1, turn.

Repeat row 3 until you are only knitting 3 sts in the middle.

Row 11: Slip 1 pwise, k4, sl&w 1, turn.

Row 12: Slip 1 pwise, k 1 st more than previous row, sl&w 1, turn.

Repeat row 12 until you can sl 1, k12, and have no more sts.

Knit second ripple

MCO a different number of sts – perhaps 11, 15, or 17. Follow the pattern you learned when making the first ripple. Hopefully the phone will ring and you'll forget exactly where you were and start knitting the ripples so they are flatter or pop up more or something else "wrong." Your scarf will be even more wonderful.

Knit more ripples until you like the length of the scarf

You know what to do.

Your scarf is the right length, so . . .

Place a marker and knit into the first ripple which is now pressing against your right needle, begging to be knit. Knit a round and purl a second round. On the following round, work ripples in the little nests waiting for them. Do not make them fit just right! A little wrong will look so much better in the end, and with this realization, your whole life may change.

By the way, here are the rules you should be following

Rule One: Never repeat the same size ripple twice in a row.

Rule Two: If something goes wrong, rejoice and dive in to see what treasures are revealed.

If you like . . .

Get into the swing of things and notice that you can accentuate the shapes by working increases and decreases. Have at it! A decrease or two in the bottom of a dip and a few increases on the hilltops as you knit back and forth could lead to – anything!

Here's Rule Three

Find something to do more or less of and see what happens.

Playtime

Notice that this is not a flat piece of knitting. It's billowy like raven-airways. Wait until you put it on. You can stick your fingers in the little mountains and pop them up and down. It's really fun.

Rolling along

If you feel moved to do another round of knit and purl just to remember what it was like to be a normal knitter, go ahead. Then keep making one never-before-seen shape after another, and when you have enough scarf to make your neck happy, bind off. If you want to do some decreases in the dips and increases in the humps to accentuate their contours, just bind off sts together for decreases or bind off things that aren't even sts for increases. Or invent another way.

I think you're done.

Yarn and design suggestions

This also looks glorious in a lush single-color yarn. But a hand-paint with colors that change several times every yard give you truly mesmerizing results. I'm still dreaming of finding just the right yarn to knit my original undulating vision: a rippling stream of hand-painted yarn in the myriad colors of running water, with rocks of mossy granite-colored yarn double-knit here and there in the stream, lightly stuffed with wool, so that they rise above the water rushing past them. Maybe a few fern fronds drifting along the edge . . . possibly a half-visible fish somewhere . . . I hope to have the yarns and time to sit and midwife this into being one day.

Seeing your Moebius experiment that didn't work freed me to trust my own mistakes. The way your messiest mistake of all turned out to lead you to so many new discoveries and designs . . . I'm no longer afraid of making mistakes.   Magic Knitting Workshop student, Friday Harbor, WA

CHAPTER ELEVEN - QUESTIONS ANSWERED, & MAGIC TRICKS

This magical being is a cria (baby llama).

Here are answers to some of the questions I hear from my inquisitive and clever workshop students. If you don't find your own burning question down below, check www.catbordhi.com, where I'll post new questions and answers.

I dropped a few stitches of the MCO. Do I have to start over again?

No, you don't. Just look at the MCO stitches that are still on your left needle, then slowly lift the dropped stitches back onto the left needle one at a time, so they are leaning the same way. Each time you lift a dropped stitch back onto the left needle, the matching stitch will appear on the cable below. They are very cooperative.

I'm a really tight knitter and the first few rounds are a struggle.

Here is where the Denise Needle Kit can help. Just use the correct needle size on the right, because the right needle is the one that determines gauge. Use a needle tip several sizes smaller on the left. This will allow your stitches to slide right along the left needle without any struggle, and your gauge ought to remain consistent. You can go down as many sizes on the left as you like. This nifty Denise Needle trick can also be used if you need a pair of circular needles for knitting the toe of the Moebius Boot, or the top of a Moebius Hat. Just snap together a pair of circular needles with the correct size needles on the right end and smaller needles on the left end, and make sure you have the correct needle size in the right hand.

How come we cast on, say 100 sts, and then you tell us to knit 200 in the first round? That doesn't make sense.

Remember how you learned to count the MCO? You counted "one" for every loop you scooped. But for every two loops you scooped, two more appeared on the cable beneath the needle. Since you knit all the way around the needle in each round, you knit twice as many stitches as you count, because all the stitches end up rotating right into place between your needles each round. Just watch and see what happens, and remember, it will work even if it remains a mystery.

Why don't we count the MCO stitches that go on the cable beneath the needle?

Think of it this way: You're making a scarf. Let's say it's 40" around. If you hung a tape measure around your neck and held the end at 40", it would match the length of your scarf; the tape and scarf could hang side by side around your neck. The tape measure has two edges, each 40" long. Our magical scarf has only one, 80" long, because it is continuous. So you cast on 80" worth of stitches because you're going to be knitting rounds which are equivalent to the 80" continuous edge. But you don't want a scarf 80" long, you want a 40" scarf. And – half of 80 is 40!

When I am halfway around my first round, and I come to the slip knot, it's hard to see where to put my needle. Do I put it into the slip knot again?

No. You only insert your needle into the slip knot on the very first stitch. When you seem to be meeting it again as the first stitch of your second half round (and your marker is on the cable directly below), what you are really meeting is the slip knot stretching up from the cable below, up and over your needle. You knit into the strand that lies over the top of your needle. Just ignore the side-by-side strands of the slip knot, and treat it like one strand of yarn behaving itself. And indeed, from now on all the stitches will behave themselves, lining up to meet you correctly mounted.

Why do I see purl bumps all the way around on my first half round of knitting?

On the Moebius highway cars drive south on the "top-side" and north on the "under-side" of the road, which happens because the road's surface runs along both one-sides of itself, being a continuous surface. I know this makes no sense but it is true nevertheless. So the purl bumps that were born when you knit along the "top-side" of the Moebius highway showed up on the "under-side," and when you appeared on the "other" one-side, there they were. Don't worry, keep driving, I mean knitting, along, and the purl bumps will be everywhere at the exact moment you meet the marker in between your needles again. It is now a one-side cobblestone highway.

I'm having a hard time getting the needle's long cable to behave. Any suggestions?

This is a common problem in the beginning. If you are using an Addi Turbo or Crystal Palace needle, just clamp the needle ends and the cable beneath them in one hand and tug the parallel cables so they even out. You may have to do this frequently in the beginning. As the Moebius width increases, the cables will begin to behave without much help from you. And once you become an old hand at Moebius knitting, you won't even have to do this, it will just happen like magic. If you are using the Denise Needle Kit, you may have the new longer cables which are just right for Moebius knitting. It *is* harder to move the stitches along a Denise cable than along an Addi Turbo or Crystal Palace. You just have to be more patient, and spend more time nudging them along.

Could you do the Moebius Cast-On by just wrapping the yarn around and around the needle and cable instead of the way you teach it?

Not really. I tried this in hopes of offering readers an alternative to the MCO, which is really the provisional cast-on applied in a new way. But I found that if you simply wrap the yarn around and around, once you begin to knit, it wants to spiral backwards and it becomes quite impossible to obtain an accurate stitch count.

Is there an easy way to undo knots in yarn skeins?

Yes, there is, funny you should ask. I just happen to have a photo of a tool called the Dental Tool, which I cannot live without.

See the bent tip at the end opposite the crochet hook? You wouldn't believe how useful it is for undoing little knots and picking up stitches and getting at things that don't want to be got. For a while they were no longer being made but now

they are available again. I warn you, if you buy one and lose it, you will be frantic. Patternworks.com has them, and I have heard that machine knitters have their own supply. I lost mine once and begged my dentist to share her dental tools with me, but when we examined her collection, there was nothing nearly as good. Then I found mine, and ordered in a lifetime supply.

I never use knots in my knitting. Do I really need to start with a slip knot?

If you want an accurate stitch count, this is the best way to insure it. If you really want to avoid the slip knot, then work a short crochet chain and use the final loop as your slip knot. After you finish the scarf, you can undo the crochet chain (maybe with your Dental Tool) and not have any knot left. I knit *auf deutsch* with a group of women and we had been calling the slip knot *das Schlippenknotten*, howling with laughter each time, until I asked Ingrid Skacel for help, and she was kind enough to phone a friend with a yarn shop in Germany to obtain the correct word, which is *die Schlinge*. If you have the book, *Knitting Languages* by Margaret Heathman (Schoolhouse Press, 1996), pencil it in.

What *does* happen if I have more than one cross of needle and cable after doing the MCO?

Well, to be quite honest, very interesting things can happen,
but you might not want them to.
You will get a cross and a half, for one thing, because the Moebius deals only in odd numbers like one, and three (three halves). While I was visiting my family over Christmas I decided to knit a Moebius magic trick involving many sleights of needle and waste yarn. I was so certain that my plan was topologically guaranteed that I boasted to everyone who stopped by for gingerbread cookies that in spite of the fact that my knitting appeared hopelessly twisted, I was sure to be successful. I completed the knitting late one evening and removed the waste yarn stitches from the surgical incisions required for sudden transformation, and lo and behold! I had a mess!

My blind topologcal faith had obscured the little fact that I had one and a half crosses of cable and needle instead of one half, and this had multiplied into twisted twisting twists where I had expected just twists. After a good night's sleep, this topological catastrophe led me directly to the creation of the little trio of one-fell-swoop Moebii you see below. The three nesting Moebii have no inside or outside and their linking arms are part of the single surface-single edge of the entire piece. This surprisingly simple pattern will appear in *The Second Treasury of Magical Knitting*.

Nesting Moebius Threesome

Is there a way to knit a one-fell-swoop Moebius without the knitting running side to side across the width of the scarf? I'd like it to run up and down.

You could do the MCO, knit a round or two – or even none, and then work a knitted-on border all the way around the single edge. It would however, meet itself at the end and you would have to graft the ends together.

What's topology?

Topology is the investigation of geometrical shapes that can be stretched and still retain their essential characteristics. It is sometimes called "rubber-sheet geometry" because topologists like to push and pull and distort the shapes as if they were made out of a rubber sheet, or, uh, knitting. The basic rule is that you cannot add a new hole or new connection to a shape. The Moebius form has the topological identity of having one surface and one edge and being non-orientable, meaning there is no point in the continuous flow from which to orient yourself. Math and knitting are kindred spirits, sharing a paradise of patterns, relationships, and that magical question: What if?

Wouldn't it be possible to make a Moebius-blocking device by taking a long width of stiff needlepoint canvas and sewing it together in a Moebius shape that matches the length of your scarf, then arrange your Moebius on its surface to dry?

That's what I thought until I remembered this imponderable mystery: You cannot lay the surfaces of two Moebii against each other. I shall not even try to explain what this is like. Just wait until you have knit two scarves, and try. Your mind will be boggled. It is similar to trying to color one side red and the other blue. Good luck.

Could you knit a Moebius from the edge in towards the spine?

I have pondered this as well and I think it could be done, although it would inevitably involve grafting together at the spine, which seems unseemly.

Are the hats still a true Moebius?

I wish you hadn't asked. I am ashamed to say that I suspect a proper topologist would scoff at them. But I'm not 100% certain. If you are a topologist, I would love to hear from you, even if you have bad news for me.

Isn't it just a technicality and not a reality that the Moebius Boots have no inside or outside?

No. It is a reality. As an architect commented upon seeing the Magical Knitting collection, "You could build a Moebius shelter, but not an enclosure."

AND NOW FOR SOME MAGIC TRICKS! JUST FOR FUN, TRY THESE THINGS:

Make a paper Moebius. Cut it in two lengthwise, along the spine all the way around. Hee hee.

Make another paper Moebius. Cut it in thirds all the way around, as if you are cutting along the yellow lines on a three-lane road that never ends. Pretty interesting, isn't it?

Now make a paper Moebius with a twist and a half, and cut it along its yellow lines. This was the topological mess I attempted to knit, using waste yarn to release the edges. It didn't work because I had a twist and a half, but I sure learned a lot! I have since knit one that worked, but I must say it lacks the charm of the one that tricked me.

Try folding a Moebius scarf in half along its length. Can you?

Now try folding a Moebius scarf this way: Fold the edge in so it just meets the spine. Can you go all the way around? Now compare this attempt with the previous one.

This is the illuminating offspring of my blind topological faith as described on page 101 and this page. There are actually two separate but intertwined scarves, only one of them a Moebius, although they were once One Moebius. The pattern will appear in The Second Treasury of Magical Knitting.

IF YOU WANT TO LEARN MORE ABOUT THE WONDERFUL MOEBIUS (AND I HOPE YOU ARE AS SMITTEN AS I AM), DO AN INTERNET SEARCH, USING THE SPELLING "MOBIUS" AS WELL.

DON'T MISS WWW.KLEINBOTTLE.COM, AND GET READY TO LAUGH YOURSELF SILLY. ISN'T THE WORLD WONDERFUL?

Preview of
The Second Treasury of Magical Knitting
bags, baskets, bowls, and cat-beds, all Moebius-derived

Moebius Basket

Jester Tentacle Bag-Turned-Hat

Striped Moebius Sling Bag

Moebius Swirl Basket

Fringed Moebius Bowl

Moebius Fanny Basket

Diamond
Moebius Sling Bag

Moebius
Basket

Jester
Tentacle Bag

Moebius
Basket

Cherry Red
Feline Bliss Bed

Moebius
Sling Bag

ALSO BY CAT BORDHI:

SOCKS SOAR ON TWO CIRCULAR NEEDLES:
A MANUAL OF ELEGANT KNITTING TECHNIQUES AND PATTERNS
Passing Paws Press, 2001

COMMENTS FROM KNITTERS:

This is so easy . . . or maybe just explained very clearly! I never thought for one instant that I couldn't do it.

I can tell that you are a teacher, because you explain things easily in several different ways.

The pictures are a life saver. I have trouble visualizing and doing what I read. But when I wasn't sure I was doing it right, I just looked at the pictures and knew what I needed to correct.

These socks really soar. My husband commented that I should have friction burns on my fingers I am knitting these up so quickly!!!

This is not just another sock pattern book, but rather a technique that is demonstrated using a variety of sock patterns. Even if you don't use the two circs method, there are some wonderfully pretty socks in this book. I also love the section on being "bilingual", translating traditional patterns to two circs.

Socks Soar **is just a work of art.** The writing and illustrations convey serenity and love. It demanded to be read twice over before embarking on the knitty gritty of the book's fundamental purpose.

CAT WRITES ABOUT SOCKS SOAR ON TWO CIRCULAR NEEDLES:

"My dream was that SOCKS SOAR would bring the magical ease of knitting on two circular needles to knitters everywhere, and I have been most gratified to see it become common knowledge. But I never dreamed the book would be a best seller! This propelled me into becoming a full-time writer, of both novels and knitting books, and I am most thankful to everyone who has made this possible."

ALSO BY CAT BORDHI:

Treasure Forest
The first of The Forest Inside trilogy

Winner of the Nautilus Award
for Young Adult Fiction

MEG SWANSEN, AUTHOR OF MANY KNITTING BOOKS AND OWNER OF SCHOOLHOUSE PRESS, WRITES:

"*Treasure Forest* came to my attention through knitting channels: the author is a knitter and knitting was to be involved in the story line; plus it was a 'children's book'. Thus two of my passions – knitting and children's literature – were to be combined. However, having been disappointed by new kids' books in the past, it was with slight skepticism that I opened this 'adventure novel.' That uncertainty melted away after the first dozen pages and I was wholly drawn into the story. Cat Bordhi's writing style is articulate and sure, and perhaps the best part is that young readers are not talked-down to. Reality and magic are entwined into a wonderful tale that moves along swiftly. As the last page is turned, a slightly bereft feeling is assuaged by the fact that this is book #1 of a trilogy. Eagerly, but patiently, I await the second book . . ."

CAT TALKS ABOUT TREASURE FOREST:

"I did not know I was writing a trilogy until I had been working on the first novel for a full year. Slowly it became clear to me that there was much more than would fit in one book, and Connie Kellough, my publisher, was delighted to hear there would be more. So I continued welcoming the pieces of the book as they came to meet me each day, setting some aside for the rest of the trilogy. It was only towards the end of writing the first book that I had a second realization: I had not started in the beginning, but the middle, and the other two books in the trilogy would come before and after the first book. And as I became more and more swept up by my magical knitting obsession, I realized that indeed, I was pregnant, in the book sense, with a set of Moebius-linked triplets. The beginning of the first novel and the end of the third novel will share a common birth, at least that's how it looks from here. Like a Moebius, the trilogy will have a continuous flow, and follow a Moebius sequence.

Following the unfolding path of a novel is astonishingly similar to following the unfurling flow of a knitting book. Both ask me to simply show up, keyboard or needles in hand, all my senses alert and willing to welcome what wants to meet me. Sometimes I think that it is because I am tame, and so the beautiful creations that populate both novels and knitting books come nibble the grass near my feet. I do not invent any of it. I simply get to be where it is, experiencing it fully so I can share it with you. And if you recognize it, if it sparks something in you, it is because it lives in you too."

Treasure Forest by Cat Bordhi
ISBN 0-9682364-8-0 (hardcover)
ISBN 0-4410136-9-4 (paperback)

Visit www.catbordhi.com for a collection of free knitting patterns

You'll find "Sara's Forest Socks" as knit by her mother in *Treasure Forest*, and a sock bookmark, along with some new Moebius designs and other things. If you'd like to knit a tree house right into a tree, learn with Sara's brother Ben, by reading the book. My web site also includes a special page on how to knit a tree house.

Vanessa Rose Ament - our model,

began dancing even before she could walk, and began singing soon after. She sings a wide range of styles from opera, to jazz, to Broadway musicals, and has performed, both singing and dancing, in over sixty shows.

Vanessa writes:

"I express myself through any type of music, because it is not the particular music that brings out my soul, but what lies beyond it that expresses it. Dance is a silent communication of feeling and emotions, which can only be expressed through this silence. Yet the music behind the dance enhances its deeper essence.

My dream is to heal people with my singing and dancing, and I believe that music has the power to heal the world. It is my dream as a performer to inspire people to believe not only in themselves and all the amazing things they are capable of doing, but also, to inspire them to have that same belief in others.

Music has the power to open us to feel love and compassion for each other. I sing and dance as an open channel of love and compassion to the world. I want to communicate that it is through the transformative power of creative expression that the world becomes a more interesting and compelling place to live, not just occasionally, but all the time."

To find out when and where Vanessa is performing, see her website: www.vanessaroseament.com

Sources

Ana-Cross Stitch

www.anacrossstitch.com
713 Commercial Avenue,
Anacortes, WA 98221
This beautiful yarn shop has
a big table and chairs for you to sit and knit,
surrounded by friendly people to answer your
questions.

Cascade Yarns

http://cascadeyarns.com
Here you'll find a painter's palette of felting yarns
(Cascade 220, in 185 colors!) as well as other
luscious yarns.

Colinette Yarns

www.colinette.com
They make the Giotto yarn that looks
likesun-kissed cedar bark.

Crystal Palace Yarns

www.straw.com
You'll find their colorful yarns in both *Treasuries*,
and they now offer their classic bamboo circular
knitting needles in a 55" length, just perfect for
Moebius knitting.

Denise Needle Kits

www.knitdenise.com 888-831-8042
I was prepared not to really like these snap-
together needles, but I love them. I prefer Addi
Turbo or Crystal Palace needles for working the
scarves, because their cables are thinner and the
yarn slides along faster, but the Denise needles
are wonderful for working the hats and boots in
this book, and many of the pieces in *A Second
Treasury of Magical Knitting*. A useful trick is to
use a much smaller tip on the left side and the
correct gauge tip on the right. Your stitches will
slide along beautifully. After all, only the right
tip determines gauge - the left tip is really just
a delivery needle. You can also use this trick to
speed up ordinary circular knitting. I never go
anywhere without my Denise Needle Kit!

Felted Knits by Bev Galeskas (Interweave Press,
2003) This excellent book offers a thorough
treatment of the idiosyncrasies of felting.

Honey Lane Farms

www.honeylanefarms.com
Honey Lane Farms raises alpacas and offers
patterns and 48 colors of pure alpaca yarns,
including clear classical jewel-tones, heathered
tones, and hand-painted yarn.

Island Wools

135 Spring Street, Friday Harbor, WA 90250
360-370-KNIT
This is my home away from home, my local
yarn shop. Just two minutes' walk from the ferry
landing, you'll find a beautiful collection of yarn,
buttons, books, and knitting tools tucked off the
main street in a peaceful courtyard, with places to
sit and knit. If you're looking for a signed copy of
one of my books, this is the place to go.

Knitopia Wools Company

1446 Johnston Rd, White Rock, B.C. V4B 3Z5
Just minutes from the Peace Arch border crossing,
Lynne Anderson offers a breath-taking selection
of delicious yarns and knitting paraphernalia. She
showcases many Canadian yarns and designers.

The Knitter's Studio

www.knittersstudio.com
725 Santa Cruz Avenue, Menlo Park, CA 94025
Wilma Peers has created an exuberant center for knitters in the middle of the Bay Area. Watch this woman and her store; she has a synergistic gift for bringing key people together to support, educate, and inspire fiber artists.

Knitting Fever

www.knittingfever.com
Distributers of Noro and Araucania yarns.

Louet Sales

www.louet.com
Louet makes Gems Merino, one of my favorite yarns, as well as Euroflax Linen.

Mountain Colors

http://mountaincolors.com
Mountain Colors yarn causes love at first sight.

Russi Sales, Inc.

http://russisales.com
Distributors of fine yarns and buttons, including Heirloom (used in the Merging Stripes Scarf) and pewter clasps (on the Lost Trail Cape).

Sivia Harding Knit Design

siviaharding@shaw.ca
http://members.shaw.ca/siviaharding
Sivia Harding offers knitted jewelry and exquisite lace shawl designs on her website, including the enchanting beaded stitch marker you see to the right.

Skacel Collection, Inc.

www.skacelknitting.com
Skacel provides yarn shops with the sleek and wonderful Addi Turbo circular needles, which come in Turbo finish brass or bamboo tips, in three Moebius sizes (40" for hats, 47" for almost everything, and 60" for really bulky yarn), as well as many of the lovely yarns used in this book.

Tahki Stacy Charles, Inc.

www.tahkistacycharles.com
Distributors of Tahki Shannon yarn.

Wool in the Woods

www.woolinthewoods.com
Best friends Anita Tostens and Missy Burns are more fun than a barrel of monkeys and run a wonderful hand-dyed yarn business. Now they are about to be authors, joined by Stephanie Blaydes Kaisler, as well. Their book, *Knitting With Hand-Dyed Yarns: 20 Stunning Projects*, will be out in November of 2004, published by Martingale. They are geniuses at combining colorways that you wouldn't think of combining, and teach color workshops to show you how. Look for their wonderful yarns and patterns in your local yarn shop.

Unicorn Books & Crafts, Inc.

www.unicornbooks.com
Distributors of Lana Grossa yarns.

Please visit www.catbordhi.com for Cat's workshop and book-signing schedule, and a posting of any errata. Please send errata to cat@catbordhi.com

ABBREVIATIONS

cdd (centered double decrease) Insert right needle into next 2 sts as if you were going to work k2tog (through both from left to right). Slip the sts to the right needle. Knit the next st on the left needle. Pass the slipped sts over the st you just knit.

k knit

k1f&b knit through front and back of same stitch

k2tog knit 2 stitches together

m1k (make 1 knit) lift strand between sts, place on needle, and knit it through the back loop

M1R (make 1 right) Lift the strand between the stitches and place it on your left needle as shown. Knit it through the front loop, which will twist it to the right.

M1L (make 1 left) Lift the strand between the stitches and place it on your left needle as shown. Knit it through the back loop, which will twist it to the left.

m1p lift strand between sts, place on needle, and purl it through the back loop

MCO (Moebius Cast-On) see page 14 for instructions, for those of you that read books backward.

p purl

p1f&b purl through front and back of same stitch

p2tog purl 2 stitches together

p3tog purl 3 stitches together

pu (pick up stitches) by inserting needle into a strand of yarn in the knitting

sl 1 kwise Slip st from the left needle to the right needle as if to knit

sl 1 pwise Slip st from the left needle to the right needle as if to purl

sl&w 1 (slip and wrap 1 stitch) Slip next st to right needle and bring yarn to front if knitting, to back if purling (that is, you move the yarn to the opposite side). Replace slipped st on left needle. When you turn the work, notice that as you bring the yarn into working position that it has wrapped itself around the slipped st like a little collar. This keeps a hole from appearing in your knitting where you turned around suddenly.

ssk (slip, slip, knit) With yarn in back, slip 1 st and then the next kwise (this changes their mounts). Replace them on left needle and knit together through back loops, from right to left. You may also work an ssk this way: With yarn in back, slip 1 stitch kwise, replace on left needle, knit it and the next stitch together from right to left through the back loops. This is faster and gives a very good result as well.

ssp (slip, slip, purl) With yarn in front, slip two stitches separately as if to knit (this changes their mounts). Replace on left needle. Insert right needle from left to right through back loops of both stitches and purl them together. If doing an ssp makes you nervous, just purl 2 sts together and be done with it. I like it though, because it makes a lovely smooth decrease.

st(s) stitch(es)

tbl through back loop

wpi wraps per inch (of yarn). See page 19 for explanation.

yo (yarn over) wrap the yarn over right needle before making next stitch.